ACCL.

"In their book, David and Rodney do a wonderful job of outlining how the little-known financial transaction of life settlement, when it fits, can make a huge difference in clients' lives. In most states usually less than a couple dozen financial professionals have both the licensing and experience to conduct these transactions for people, and David and Rodney are two of the best. Besides covering the technical side of the transaction, they explain how this tool can improve the lives of those who use them. I highly recommend this book for anyone considering what to do with a life policy that has outlived its need or that has become unaffordable."
—Lawrence J. Rybka JD, CFP®
CEO of Valmark Financial Group, co-author of *Life Insurance 10X* and *Tools and Techniques of Life Settlements*

"Everyone can benefit from a coach to help them reach their full potential in business and in life. The same holds true when it comes to our finances. In their book *In the Know*, David Rosell and Rodney Cook expertly coach individuals—as well as the financial professionals who represent them—on how to take advantage of life settlements and trade superfluous life insurance policies for potentially life-changing profit."
—Dan Sullivan
Co-founder and president of Strategic Coach®

"David and Rodney bring to light a fourth option for clients and their advisors to consider when circumstances have rendered life insurance policies unnecessary or unwanted. Via their unique and real-life stories, they explain life settlements, making a complex decision and process simple and easy to understand. Knowing alternatives is one thing; possessing the ability to demonstrate and implement appropriate actions is another."
—Kenneth R. Ehinger
Former senior executive of M Financial Group, Lincoln Financial Group and National Life Group

"After 40 years in the life insurance profession, I've assisted thousands of clients in acquiring policies at the best pricing classification possible and encouraged them to keep the policy for their lifetime. Occasionally, life events change those plans which force clients to settle their policy. In David and Rodney's thorough and well written book, they explain how you can benefit from another option to settle your life insurance policy that, when professionally managed, could bring you unexpected value when it's needed most."
—Phil Harriman, CLU, ChFC
Founding Partner of Lebel & Harriman, 2007 International President of MDRT (Million Dollar Round Table), former Maine State Senator

"Whether you are an expert in life settlements or hearing about them for the first time, this book is relevant for you. Rosell and Cook have penned a concise, entertaining, and informative read on how you might be able to unlock the hidden value of life insurance you no longer need."
—Caleb J. Callahan, CFP
President of Valmark Financial Group

"The best financial planning is flexible, adaptable, and impactful. This requires a planning process that is dynamic, regularly updated, and responsive to changing laws, objectives, risks, opportunities, and family dynamics. It goes without saying that the best life insurance professionals don't just help their clients buy a strategically designed policy, but they also have expertise in selling existing policies, as may be necessary and helpful as an asset within the plan. David and Rodney are true planning and life insurance professionals who have this important expertise, as demonstrated by this clear and extremely helpful book they've written. I can't recommend it enough. Read it, for your own benefit and your family's."
—Ron Ware, JD, CFP
CEO of Trove Private Wealth, author of *You Can Do More That Matters*

"David Rosell and Rodney Cook have taken the complex financial concept of life settlements and explain it to readers through their use of storytelling. However, their stories are about REAL clients and ACTUAL transactions that have occurred. How do you turn life insurance from an uncorrelated financial asset to cash for clients when they no longer have a need for it? Read on."
—Julian H. Good, Jr. CLU, ChFC, AEP
Founder of Good Financial Group, 2011 International President of MDRT (Million Dollar Round Table)

In The Know is a unique resource that brings new light and understanding to the financial opportunity of a life settlement. This powerful work will be extremely helpful to people who are wondering what to do with their expensive life insurance policies that have become unaffordable. With David and Rodney on your team, you're sure to understand your options and make a wise, profitable decision.
—Greg Salciccioli
Founder and CEO of Coachwell and Coachwell Capital, author of *The Enemies of Excellence*

Lawrence J. Rybka, Kenneth R. Ehinger, Phil Harriman, Caleb J. Callahan, Ron Ware and Julian H. Good are associated persons of Valmark Securities.

IN THE KNOW

Turning Your Unneeded Life Insurance Policy Into Serious Cash

David Rosell and Rodney Cook

In The Know
Turning Your Unneeded Life Insurance Policy Into Serious Cash

© 2022 by David Rosell and Rodney Cook

ISBN: 9781662862953

All rights reserved. No part of this book may be reproduced in whole or in part without written permission from the publishers, except by reviewers who may quote brief excerpts in connection with a review in a newspaper, magazine, or electronic publication; nor may any part of this book be reproduced, stored in a retrieval system, or transmitted in any form or by any means electronic, mechanical, photocopying, recording, or other, without written permission from the publisher.

The advice provided by the author is based on personal and professional experience in dealing with issues surrounding financial planning and investing; however, it is not a substitute for paid professional guidance. The studies and statistics quoted are, to the best of the author's knowledge and belief, accurate. This book is sold without warranties of any kind, express or implied, and both the author and publisher disclaim any liability, loss, or damage caused by its contents.

Cover design by Lieve Maas

Published by
MCP Books
2301 Lucien Way Suite 415
Maitland, FL 32751

DEDICATIONS

Heather Ewing, you are better than fiction. Thank you for your endless love and support. Here's to a lifetime of love and adventures. **To Sophie and Jack**, I am incredibly honored to be your father and so proud of the stellar young adults you have become.

Much love,
David

Thank you to my wife **Kira** and son **Makaih** for your continuous support, patience and unwavering love. **To my parents**, gracias de todo corazón. ¡Wepa!

In gratitude,
Rodney

ACKNOWLEDGEMENTS

In The Know is the result of many people's time, energy, commitment, and expertise. We would like to express our gratitude and appreciation for those people who have supported and encouraged us throughout this two-year ride, notably…

Emma James, the world's greatest *Integrator* and guiding light of our practice.

Linden Gross, whose guidance and coaching enabled us to take what could be a rather dry subject and make this book an educational and fun read. Our professional relationship has turned into a beautiful friendship over the past decade.

Lieve Maas, who combined creativity and passion to create this most handsome book design.

Elizabeth Crane, a talented copy editor who meticulously reread our manuscript numerous times to ensure excellence.

James Dawson, **Michael Michlitsch** and **Heath Smargiasso,** whose knowledge and capabilities added so much to our book. It's always an honor to team up with the three of you.

Our clients. We thank you for the confidence and trust you have placed in us to guide your financial futures. You are our motivation day in and day out, year in and year out.

All you CPAs, attorneys, trust advisors, financial advisors, and insurance agents, who entrust us to help your clients make informed and educated decisions.

Lastly, to you the reader. We hope you learn how to turn something of little to no value into a significant nest egg and live the life you have always imagined in your exciting years of financial independence.

SERENDIPITY

FUN COUPONS

NEPAL

MCKENZIE RIVER

LES BROWN

Preface

SEIZE THE DAY
AND THE OPPORTUNITY

> *I am a firm believer in serendipity—all the random pieces coming together in one wonderful moment, when suddenly you see what their purpose was all along.*
> —David Levithan

You—or your client—are making the most of life's golden years, which are hopefully proving to be the best phase of your life. Early on, ensuring that dependents would be taken care of no matter what or safeguarding against financial downturns made sense. But now, that might no longer be the case. Or maybe you no longer have to worry about concerns like estate taxes upon your passing, insuring your business partner, or about any number of other reasons that compelled you to buy life insurance years ago. So why are you still hanging onto that costly life insurance policy when you could trade it in for a pile of fun coupons?

Make that a mountain of fun coupons.

We're about to introduce you to life settlements: trading in life insurance you no longer want or need, and that has probably gotten increasingly expensive over the years, for potentially way more than the policy's cash surrender value. Now that's what we call a good fortune.

It all starts with taking action after recognizing the opportunity. That's what we (your authors, David and Rodney) have both done throughout our lives.

Meet David (in his own words)

Coincidence. Destiny. Karma. Luck. Fate. Good fortune. These words all describe the opportunity presented in this book, which just might be your ticket to ride. They're also all words that describe how I got to this point in life. However, the word that I think best describes it all is *serendipity*.

> **Serendipity: noun. Ser·en·dip·i·ty / ser-ən-ˈdi-pə-tē /**
> **Def:** luck that takes the form of finding valuable or pleasant things that are not looked for. They found each other by pure *serendipity*.

This has been a favorite word of mine since I first learned about it through the writings of Dr. Wayne Dyer in the late 1980s. Life certainly has its ups and downs for everyone. While I'm no exception, much of my life has been guided by unexpected, good happenings.

Serendipity #1: Sealing my way to success

I never would have imagined that helping my dad seal coat our driveway at the age of 15 would forever change the direction of my life and be the catalyst to living a life of hard work, adventure, and serendipity. When our next-door neighbor saw me sealing our driveway, he asked me if I would do his. I made $25 on that scorching, humid July day in 1984. By the time I headed off to college three years later, the idea to turn this into a business had proliferated into a couple of employees.

We were seal coating 100 driveways at $75 a pop by then, but that wasn't enough. Each summer, I would return to grow my business. I started advertising in newspapers, sending out mass mailers with coupons and placing professional signs in the ground after completing each job. I was determined to turn a blue-collar business into a white-collar business. We began calling our customers clients. As you might imagine, not a single client wanted even a speck of this messy black material on their homes, so to set us apart from the competition, I started providing a written guarantee stating that if there was a drop of the sealer on their home, garage doors, sidewalk, lawn, or even on the street, they would get the job for free.

My plan was so successful that it soon became hard to keep up with demand, even though I now had four guys working for me. I continued to raise our prices to a fee commensurate with the rise in the quality of our work, and we continued to get busier. I invested in a second vehicle to increase efficiency and began letting my crews handle the driveway sealing while I drove around providing estimates, checking on our various jobs, and running the overall business. We seal coated a couple hundred driveways during the summer of 1988, prompting our local newspaper to run a front-page story titled "19-Year-Old Entrepreneur Seals His Success."

Most college students don't experience that kind of business success. And most kids would have focused on what the money they had earned could buy them. But thanks to my grandma and father, I wasn't most kids.

David Rosell (age 19) with his newest driveway sealing truck, purchased at a police auction.

SERENDIPITY #2: FINANCIAL FOUNDATION

I will always remember the day my Grandma Ruth changed how I thought about money. I was 19 years old, and with great enthusiasm, I showed her the brochure of the brand-new black Honda Prelude I was planning to finance. She knew how to communicate with a teenager, so she told me how proud she was that I had the means to purchase a new car at my age (even though the bank would actually be buying it for me).

"You'll have the nicest car of all of your friends," she said, right before she shared with me a chart that explained what an IRA is and the financial impact it could have on my life. The illustration showed that if I invested $2,000, the maximum IRA contribution at the time, between the ages of 19 and 27, assuming the account compounded at 10 percent per year, I would be a millionaire by age 65 even if I never placed additional contributions into the account. Not only that, but I would have more money than that if I started investing $2,000 per year at the age of 27 and did so each and every year until age 65. This is when I truly learned to appreciate what Albert Einstein reportedly considered the world's eighth wonder: the compound interest formula. My grandma taught me the difference between working for money and having money work for me. I never did buy that car. Instead, I started my IRA, a decision that would change my life.

Several years later, as my business income grew, I decided to invest more. Unlike most 20-somethings, I had already begun to accumulate significant investment savings, the result of my father teaching me that the tougher I am on myself today, the easier life will be on me later. This sounded good to me as I had so many dreams to realize. Dad taught me about the tax advantages of retirement accounts, and this excited me so much that I started sharing that information with my employees, hoping they would buy into the concept of paying themselves first and experience the effects of compound interest. Friends and family members began approaching me with investment questions. These experiences forever changed my perspective on finance.

Serendipity #3: Not all who wander are lost

By the time I had graduated college, my company was seal coating over 300 driveways per summer. As fall approached and all my friends started to send out resumes looking for jobs in the business arena, I decided I would explore the world during the six months that Mother Nature forced me to shut down operations. I told my parents I would travel for the winter, come home to run the business one more summer, and then find a "real job."

With a backpack, a one-man tent, and a small gas stove, I decided to head to Fiji, New Zealand, and Australia since they were English-speaking countries. Besides, I had always been intrigued by the nature Down Under. By the following year, however, I still wasn't ready to settle down. Instead, once the weather got cold after another summer running my driveway business, I turned my focus to Southeast Asia. After six months abroad, spending a month in six different countries, I returned home to my business.

I had absolutely no idea at that time that I would end up running my business for eight more years. By the time I sold the company at age 30, we were sealing 1,200 driveways a summer and had expanded into power-washing decks and siding to take advantage of the rainy days when we could not seal coat. Each year when the cold hit, I packed my bags and traveled for six months.

During the decade I ran my seal coating business after graduating college, I spent a month in 65 different countries on six continents. Thumb, bus, train, plane, and even hiking got me through South America, Africa, Australia, Europe, and the Far East.

My annual sojourns around the world helped shape me into the person I've become and would eventually prompt me to write books that combine two of my core passions—international adventure travel and helping guide people regarding their financial future.

Over the years, I have learned that experiencing serendipity may have a lot to do with being in the right place at the right time. However, I believe many more of these opportune events happen because of attitude, deliberate creation, the Law of Attraction, and taking action. Ski-film pioneer Warren Miller, who has traveled the globe in search of the wild steep and deep, has always had the uncanny ability to capture the adventure, wonder, and beauty that is skiing and that is life. He ended each and every one of his movies with the same statement, which impacts me just as strongly today as it did in my youth: *If you don't do it this year, you'll be one year older when you do.*

David Rosell in Annapurna, Nepal, 1992.

Serendipity #4: Money Man

By now, you probably understand that my life up to that point had been about cashing in my fun coupons. Yet serendipity means nothing if you don't act on it. To this day, I know the shape of my life has so much to do with the financial acumen I developed early on, thanks to those two primary sources of inspiration, Dad and Grandma. They taught me how to be in the know when it came to handling money because I had started to make significant profits at a young age, and failure was not an option. This paved the way for my driveway business, which eventually led to my international explorations. The culmination of all these experiences would lead to the second phase of my professional life.

I knew my next calling was to help people discover the lessons I had learned from my grandmother and father and share the knowledge I had acquired from watching my retirement accounts begin to grow. People do not need to do anything extraordinary to become financially independent. They just need to do some ordinary things (like saving a portion of every paycheck) extraordinarily well (at every pay period). Over two decades, I've focused on helping successful people at or near retirement plan their financial future so they can live the life they have always imagined.

While this continues to be a deep passion, I'm excited to share with you my latest calling: helping individuals like yourself—as well as estate planning attorneys, CPAs, and insurance agents—discover and uncover the potential benefits of life settlements. My business partner and co-author Rodney and I know that when used appropriately with the right people in the right circumstances, a life settlement can significantly impact a person's life in so many positive ways. I'm hoping that once you're *In the Know* about this financial strategy, this may prove to be a serendipitous day for you and the first day of the rest of your financial life.

David Rosell

Meet Rodney (in his own words)

Serendipity plays a role in all our lives. How much depends in part on setting the stage to make it happen.

Grabbing your future

My family and I had driven from Los Angeles to Bend, Oregon, a town with only 80,000 residents at that time. The historic cabin we stayed in had a picture-perfect view of the Sisters—three snowcapped volcanic peaks—and Mount Bachelor, Bend's local ski resort. I woke up before sunrise as the morning sun cast an alpenglow across the horizon. I had an intuitive feeling this would end up being one of the most important days of my life. I was right.

I remember that morning in 2016 as if it were yesterday. I had laid out my clothes the night before, as I always do before a big day. During breakfast, I prepared my notes and questions. I was ready to interview for the position of director of financial planning at Rosell Wealth Management.

My wife and I were thrilled at the thought of moving back to our home state of Oregon, where we both had grown up. When she discovered this job posting, she strongly encouraged me to apply. I did, and the rest is history. Thank you, Kira.

After meeting David, I immediately knew this job was for me. We spent the entire day together learning about each other, his unique practice and what my role would potentially be.

Serendipity 2.0

The most profound moment of the daylong interview came during the morning session. David asked me, "If you could have lunch with anyone in the world, dead or alive, who would it be and why?"

Usually, I need some time for this type of arbitrary question, yet one person immediately came to mind. Without hesitation, I said with confidence, "Mr. Les Brown." Les and my father were the only men in my life at this time who had truly inspired me to be the best version of myself.

Have you ever heard of Les Brown? Well, let me tell you. He is one of the most impressive motivational speakers in the country. At his height, he sold out the Georgia Dome, which seats more than 70,000 people. His story, combined with his prowess and humor, makes him one of the all-time greats. The fact that he is Black and I could identify with him added to my affinity for him. His powerful quotes continue to motivate me to be the best person and financial planner I can be.

Of all his quotes, this is the one that impacts me the most:

> *If you want a thing bad enough to go out and fight for it, to work day and night for it, to give up your time, your peace*

and sleep for it. If all that you dream and scheme is about it, and life seems useless and worthless without it. If you gladly sweat for it and fret for it and plan for it and lose all your terror of the opposition for it. If you simply go after that thing that you want with all your capacity, strength and sagacity, faith, hope and confidence, and stern pertinacity. If neither cold, poverty, famine, nor gout, sickness nor pain, of body and brain, can keep you away from the thing that you want. If dogged and grim you besiege and beset it, with the help of God, YOU WILL GET IT!

Rodney Cook with Les Brown, Bend, Oregon, 2019.

If you had told me on that first day I met David that he would be introducing me to Les Brown just two years later and that I would have an entire hour alone to get acquainted with him, I would have concluded that you were dreaming. Instead, that moment will remain one of the most powerful and memorable experiences of my life. His compassionate words of wisdom still encourage me to keep moving forward and to stay hungry for life's adventures.

Answering the Call

The five years in Bend that followed delivered on everything I had hoped for. I was productive and, even more importantly, happy. Then, on May 11, 2020, I awoke to the headlines of Ahmaud Arbery being gunned down as he jogged through a neighborhood while the shooter's father stood on the bed of a truck watching, pistol in hand.

This was just the start of a sequence of similar events over the following weeks where innocent Black individuals experienced violent deaths. Viewing these horrific acts on television and witnessing the lack of justice shook me like nothing I had ever experienced. I became physically ill, and I struggled to get through my daily activities. I would find myself bursting into tears throughout the following days. This was no longer about fearing for myself but for my 15-year-old son. How could I explain to him that he might be treated differently or even killed for the color of his skin? How would I be able to protect him?

I knew that David would be supportive of the emotions I was contending with; however, I was a bit surprised when he suggested I put my thoughts and feelings on paper and write a letter. David was the writer in the practice, not me. So, I pushed my discomfort aside and poured out all the emotion that was suffocating me. This letter would later be published in newspapers throughout the state and make it to the governor's office in Salem, Oregon, which led to my sitting on Oregon's Equity and Recovery Council. The outpouring of support from my community amazed me. I learned firsthand that day that you make your own luck by following your heart and taking action.

Turning a challenge into an opportunity

While my letter helped put me back on my feet that spring, Covid was doing its best to yank them out from under me again. By spring 2020, the world had gone into lockdown due to the global pandemic. A two-week national shutdown turned into a month and then several months and eventually more than two years.

During those days filled with fear of the unknown, many people, myself included, began to turn to Mother Nature to heal our angst and loneliness. The outdoors has always been a grounding force in my life. My mother, an accomplished runner, was responsible for my love of running outside. She had been recruited to UC Davis to run track on scholarship, an especially impressive feat considering that she grew up in Puerto Rico, running on a dirt track.

While I've always enjoyed running, Covid had sidelined me for too long. Finally, after a three-mile run conclusively demonstrated that I was out of shape and needed a motivational force to get me back to the physical condition I was accustomed to, I decided to call my mom and ask her a question that would certainly get her attention. When she picked up the phone, the first words out of my mouth were, "Do you want to run an ultra?"

I was talking about an ultramarathon.

Silence on the other end.

"It's only a 50K (31 miles), and there's more downhill than uphill," I said hurriedly.

That's when she spoke up and reminded me that I had never run anything longer than a half marathon (13.1 miles) and that she had undergone four knee surgeries and had just turned 60.

"Just think about it," I urged.

My mom is very competitive and never backs down from a challenge. She called me back five minutes after hanging up. "How do I sign up?" she asked.

YES! I have always been able to count on my mom to show up and be by my side throughout life's events.

The ultramarathon I had in mind was the McKenzie River Trail Run, one of Oregon's oldest ultramarathons. This breathtaking trail traverses lush old-growth forests and ancient lava fields, and winds past lakes so clean you can see more than 100 feet to the bottom. After snaking through forest floor carpeted in an emerald green of thick moss and ferns, the McKenzie River crashes 140 feet over a lava cliff to form the stunning Sahalie Falls. It would be the epic trail run of my life.

Rodney Cook crossing the finish line with his mother, Melinda Cook. McKenzie River Trail, 2021.

After months of training, race day finally arrived. All I could think of on that cool, foggy September morning was, *What did I get us into? Who in their right mind pays for the privilege of running 31 miles for fun?*

The bang of the starting gun jolted us, and we were off. I chased my mom through miles of Douglas fir trees up to six feet in diameter that reminded me of California's redwoods and giant sequoias. It felt as though the birds were singing for us. We were indeed one with nature, and I was in my happy place with mom right next to me.

Every six miles, an aid station allowed us to fill up our CamelBak packs with water, eat our protein bars, and down our fruit pouches. The volunteers helping to put on the race loved that we were a mother-son combo and that my mother, 20-plus years my senior, was not only sticking by my side but, a couple of times, *she* had to wait for *me* to catch up.

As we finally ran down the last rocky hill, 30 miles behind us, my tired legs became fresh again. By the time I saw the finish line, volunteers cheered us along. My mom and I locked hands and crossed the finish line together, raising our arms as if we had just won the Boston marathon. We looked at each other, and a single thought ricocheted through my mind. *We did it!*

Would I have ever attempted an ultra had Covid not propelled me to find a new, safe outlet or had my mom not agreed to join me? I seriously doubt it. In the end, however, this global health challenge inspired an achievement of a lifetime. Why share that experience in a book about life settlements? Because a life settlement could turn out to be your chance of a lifetime.

Rodney Cook

Is this your chance?

All too often, especially when life gets in the way, we don't see opportunities that are right in front of us. So, what if we told you that something you don't think you want anymore and have assumed is valueless could potentially be worth some serious cash?

Life insurance can be a lifeline. There's nothing better than knowing that you can protect your loved ones even after you're gone. If we're lucky, however, we outlive the need for the powerful impact that life insurance can have. If that's your story—or your client's—this book is for you. We're about to explain how you can turn a superfluous and often expensive life insurance policy into the kind of money that could redefine your golden years. We'll tell you right now that the information in this book is not directed to young people looking at many years ahead. Let's face it. They have plenty of options, right? It's about time for those who have lived long to prosper.

- CARRIBEAN CRUISE
- PORTLAND INT'L. RACEWAY
- MT. HOOD SKI AREA
- MOUNT TAM
- GYM

Chapter 1

DON'T NEED, DON'T WANT?

Your Life Insurance Policy Could Pay Off Now

Fun is like life insurance; the older you get, the more it costs.
—Kin Hubbard

Don't you hate it when you've spent a ton of money on something you don't need? That can feel even worse if you're still paying for it.

Does this remind you of your life insurance policy?

I know. You're tempted to just walk away since it no longer serves you. But what if you could sell it?

Shockingly, up to 90 percent of life insurance policies[1] never pay a death benefit. Instead, they expire, lapse, or are surrendered. In short, most people who have purchased life insurance get little to nothing for the money they've spent. How much sense does that make? None. You wouldn't want to walk away from a Lamborghini just because you didn't drive it anymore. No, you'd sell it. Hello!

So, if you need (or want) money—and who doesn't—you may be able to do precisely the same thing with a life insurance policy that has outlived its purpose.

People like us pay our life insurance premiums each year to protect our loved ones or business partners. We are true proponents of life insurance. But let's be real, this is a policy you hope doesn't get used anytime soon. If you're lucky, you will outlive the need for your life insurance policy. But what happens when:

- This policy that you have been paying for is no longer needed or you just can't afford the often-rising premiums?
- Your children are no longer dependents, and you've built up enough wealth to make sure your family is taken care of for the rest of their lives?
- You and your business partner have sold your company, and the insurance policies you had in place to protect each other and your families are no longer wanted?
- Then there are all the families who purchased policies to cover the expected estate taxes upon the second spouse's passing, and now federal exemptions have increased so much that only 0.1 percent of Americans will have to pay a federal estate tax.[2]

"I was paying premium on a policy originally intended for estate taxes, but I no longer have the tax liability."

These are just some of a slew of potential situations where life insurance played a pivotal role in significantly leveraging money to provide security and peace of mind, but now the need for such coverage has diminished or evaporated altogether.

Most people believe they have only three options for their now unwanted and unneeded life insurance policies. They include:

1. Keep the policy and continue paying the increased premiums.
2. Decrease the death benefit of the policy to maintain an affordable premium.
3. Let the policy lapse and receive any potential cash value that has accumulated if it's a permanent policy.

What if there was a fourth option that might benefit you or your client much more? Would you like to learn how you could potentially profit from the sale of your life insurance policy? We're going to introduce you to a strategy that insurance companies do not want you to know about.

We feel you should be in the know about a relatively unknown yet powerful option: life settlements. Your home, automobile, boat, investment portfolio, investment real estate, and business interests are all considered capital assets. However, most people aren't aware that your life insurance policies are also considered a capital asset—an asset that may have significant value.

How can this be? I hear you asking yourself.

The answer starts with getting acquainted with what a life settlement is and what it's not.

So, what is a life settlement?

A life settlement is the sale of an existing life insurance policy, often to a third-party institutional investor. These investors on what we call the secondary market often include pension funds, hedge funds, or banks. The policy is put up for sale for more than its cash surrender value and less than its death benefit.

In such a transaction, the policy owner sells the policy in exchange for a lump sum cash payment. The policy owner is often the insured but can also include entities such as businesses or an irrevocable life insurance trust.

Once the policy is sold to the institutional investor, they become the policy's owner. It is now their responsibility to make all the premium payments moving forward. In return, they will eventually receive the death benefit upon the insured's death. These institutional investors purchase many different life insurance policies to diversify their holdings. It is helpful to know that the purchased policies are owned in large blind pools with many other policies. This helps to assure client confidentiality.

In addition, the investors participate in the performance of the grouping of numerous policies. You can think of it as similar to a mutual fund portfolio where the investors are less concerned about each individual equity holdings they own and more focused on the overall performance of their pool of assets. Even though the institutional investors who purchase unwanted policies do not have access to an insured's personal information, reputable companies service these portfolios and keep confidential records of the names and contact information needed to track an insured's health.

Although it's possible to sell a policy to an individual investor, this is not a standard or recommended practice. An individual investor would need to have a one-on-one relationship with the insured and policy owner, and confidentiality would not be possible. For obvious reasons, we feel strongly that an insured should never sell their life insurance policy to any individual who stands to profit from the insured's death. No one wants to see a Tony Soprano get involved with such a beneficial solution for unwanted life insurance policies.

"We need to ask ourselves . . 'what would Tony Soprano do ? '. . "

WHAT A LIFE SETTLEMENT IS NOT

Speaking of Tony, you may be relieved to know that a life settlement is not a viatical settlement. Viatical settlements arose as the AIDS epidemic took hold in the 1980s. In a typical viatical settlement, the insured is terminally ill and has a life expectancy of 24 months or less. An example is a father who owns a $250,000 life insurance policy on his life. If he maintains the policy, his family will receive $250,000 in tax-free proceeds from the insurance company upon the father's inevitable and rapidly approaching death. What if the family does not have the economic means to fulfill the family dream of visiting Europe together and seeing the Eiffel Tower before his passing? Investors may offer the family $150,000, allowing the family to travel together. In this case, the investor would collect the entire death benefit upon his passing.

Although there are positive outcomes in viatical settlements, there is often too much room for others to take advantage of vulnerable policyholders. Unlike viaticals, life settlements involve policyholders who may not be terminally ill but generally have a life expectancy of between two and 15 years instead of just 24 months. Life settlements also tend to involve policies with higher net death benefits than viatical settlements.

What's in it for you or your client?

The bottom line is that unneeded and sometimes financially burdensome life insurance policies can often be sold for a heck of a lot more than you would get by simply letting them go. Of course, like most major financial transactions, this should only be considered after a thorough analysis of the pros and cons of retaining the policy versus selling or surrendering it. But suppose a life insurance policy is no longer necessary. In that case, a life settlement could result in the policy owner receiving a more significant amount than if the policy was allowed to lapse or was surrendered for its cash surrender value.

The most effective way to get you in the know on life settlements is to share actual case studies. Before we share these sometimes surprising stories, it's important to know the following:

- All client names have been changed to protect confidentiality.
- The gross offer we procure for our clients is always reduced by commissions and expenses related to the sale.
- Every client's experience is unique, and there is no guarantee that a life settlement will generate an offer greater than the current cash surrender value. In such cases, the client can always surrender their policy to the carrier if the coverage is no longer needed.
- This material is intended for informational purposes only and should not be construed as legal or tax advice or investment recommendations. Please consult a qualified attorney, tax advisor, investment professional, or insurance agent about the issues discussed herein.
- Although all the life settlement financial details in these stories use exact numbers, the names of the individuals and details about their lives have been changed to protect their privacy.

Okay, so now that we're done with all that, let's meet some people who, with a little (or a lot of) help from our Valmark Financial Group team, have made life settlements work for them.

Tackling the Increased Cost of Insurance

After teaching second grade in Ohio for years, Nancy DeRose and her husband Charles, who spent his career at Proctor &

Gamble but is now deceased, retired to San Rafael, California. Over the next 15 years, Nancy focused on learning about the birds in this new place she now calls home. Birdwatching is a popular hobby for many people; however, Nancy, who refers to herself as a twitcher or birder, takes it to an entirely new level of passion. She's so serious about birds, we believe she could go head-to-head with most ornithologists.

Not far from her home is one of her favorite places on the planet—Mount Tamalpais State Park, which, as a long-time Marin County local, she refers to as Mt. Tam. Although one can drive nearly to the top, 79-year-old Nancy still prefers to hike in a few miles on this 13-mile loop. Nothing excites her more than getting a photo of a Hutton's vireo, a wrentit, or a pygmy nuthatch. She'll then go home and use the shot to paint a watercolor extravaganza.

Nancy's other passion is her only child—her son, Ron, a successful orthopedist—and her two grandchildren, ages 20 and 17. Next year, she wants to take them all, along with Ron's wife, on the Royal Clipper. This five-masted tall ship is listed in Guinness World Records as the largest full-rigged sailing ship in the world. Her 42 sails require a crew of 20 to get the 439-foot clipper ship doing 17 knots on sail power alone.

On this trip, Nancy can combine the two most important elements of her life, her loved ones and her beloved birds. She plans to visit the bird sanctuaries of the West Indies while her family soaks up the Caribbean sun. But that's going to take money.

Nancy would have had enough to pull off the trip, but she found out that her insurance company was increasing the premiums on the $4 million universal life insurance policy that she and Charles had purchased in 1995 for estate planning purposes. It turns out that, for Nancy to maintain the policy through her life expectancy, her planned premium would increase from $44,000 to $106,000.

That's not just a premium hike, that's more like an ultramarathon without any of the associated pleasure.

While Nancy might have just been able to afford the increased premiums if she scaled back, she certainly would never be able to afford to take her family on this dream vacation. Then she realized that she no longer needed the policy for estate planning purposes. The new tax laws had raised the federal exemption level to more than $12 million. Even if that dropped back down to $5 million in 2026, as it is expected to do, she would be fine. So why pay for an expensive policy she no longer needed?

Instead of simply walking away or surrendering her policy for its cash value, Nancy consulted her accountant, who turned to us for help. We provided the pair with four options: surrender the policy, reduce the death benefit, pay the increased premiums, or the fourth option—sell the policy. Instead of surrendering the policy, Nancy, whose life expectancy at that point was roughly six to ten years, took our recommendation and decided to pursue selling the policy through a life settlement.

Our life settlement team worked with multiple providers through a professional bidding process and negotiated a settlement offer, resulting in a total gross offer of $1,521,000, or two and a half times the cash surrender value. That's a heck of a lot more than the policy's $640,602 cash surrender value. And boy, that extra $880,398 she grossed will sure finance one heck of a family/birding holiday.

An all-too-often-unknown option

In most states, insurance carriers are not required to tell the owners of life insurance policies that they have the option to sell their policy instead of lapsing or surrendering it. Therefore, it's the financial advisor's responsibility to educate clients regarding the life settlement option. Unfortunately, most insurance agents, financial planners, CPAs, and estate planning attorneys we've come across have been unaware of such solutions for unwanted life insurance policies.

According to a 2015 survey by Wealth Management, 40 percent of financial advisors,[3] by their own admission, know little to nothing about life settlements, which helps explain why only 11 percent have ever recommended a life settlement to their clients.[4]

Not surprisingly, studies show that more than 50 percent of seniors had no idea they could sell their policies.[5] Of those, nearly 90 percent who lapsed or surrendered their policies back to insurance carriers would have considered selling the policy had they known that life settlements existed.[6] Luckily, Nancy was introduced to us before she surrendered her policy.

How do life settlements work?

Okay, let's review some basics and introduce a few others.

The buyers of life settlements—often referred to as life settlement companies or providers—can hold the policies to maturity and collect the net death benefits. Others will bundle many purchased policies together and resell the assortment of policies to hedge funds or other investors.

The people who sell their policies do so in exchange for a lump-sum payment. The amount they will receive in the secondary market depends on a number of factors, including their age, their health, and their policy's terms and conditions.

In addition to paying you a lump sum for your policy, the buyer agrees to pay any additional premiums that might be required to support the cost of the policy for as long as you live. In exchange, the buyer will receive the death benefit when you die. And if they let the policy lapse, that's on them, not on you, since you will have already received payment in exchange for your policy.

After selling your life insurance policy, all you have to worry about is enjoying that money and keeping the policy's buyer waiting as long as possible to collect the death benefit proceeds.

ARE YOU A POTENTIAL LIFE SETTLEMENT CANDIDATE?

Often when policyholders first learn about settlements and see how lucrative they can be, their eyes light up, and thoughts of newfound funds for a Class A motorhome or vacation home come to mind. So, let's look at who potentially qualifies for such a strategy.

Here are the prerequisites:

- The insured's age is typically 65 and older, unless facing a life-shorting condition.
- Their life expectancy is 15 years or less.
- There has been a decline in health from the original policy issue.
- The life insurance policy has a net death benefit of $250,000 or more (there's no maximum).
- The policy owner can be an individual, trust, or corporation.
- Life insurance policies can be universal life, guaranteed universal life, survivorship universal life, variable universal life, and convertible term. Flexible premium policies like universal life are more favored by buyers because they can readily adjust the premiums going forward.

- The annual premium should be 5 percent of the death benefit (or less), and the cash surrender value should be 15 percent of the death benefit (or less).

A settlement is only possible when the policy's market value exceeds the cash surrender value. Key factors in determining the market value of a policy are the death benefit, the cost of future premiums, and the insured's life expectancy.

As you might imagine, even though it's tough to think about, life expectancy is the key component in determining the market value of a life settlement transaction. The lower the premiums and the shorter the life expectancy, the higher the selling price. Conversely, the greater the amount of premiums that need to be paid and the longer the investor must wait for the death benefit, the lower the policy value.

Let's flip that notion around and look on the positive side. If you don't need the life insurance policy, it can really feather your nest during this chapter of your life.

Missed life settlement opportunities

If you're the owner of a life insurance policy that's no longer required or wanted but aren't sure what to do about that, you're not alone. Unfortunately, as we previously shared, more than half of all seniors have no idea they might be able to sell their life insurance policies. That potentially explains why each year, more than $112 billion in life insurance (face value) is allowed to lapse or is surrendered by individuals over age 65. That's $112 billion with a B![7] That only partially explains why so many people are walking away from the profit they could potentially collect from a life settlement.

Enter life insurance companies, who make far less money when they have to pay out a death benefit than when a policy is allowed to lapse or when it's surrendered. But, of course, that's in all likelihood not going to happen if that policy is sold to an investor. As a result, insurance companies don't exactly make it easy to obtain a life settlement.[8] Not only do they refrain from explaining the life settlement option to policy owners (even threatening to fire those sales agents who do mention it), they lobby for state laws that could restrict or even shut down the life settlement market.

But that's far from the only impediment. The more significant issue gets back to plain old lack of knowledge. As we've seen, not only do policy owners not realize that they can potentially sell those unwanted life insurance policies, but their financial advisors don't realize this either.

Luckily, that wasn't the case for Donald Jenkins.

Higher and higher

Like Nancy DeRose, Donald Jenkins's premiums on his $1.3 million universal life policy, which was owned by a limited partnership, had soared, a story that's all too common these days.

Donald had spent his career working for Delta Airlines in Atlanta before retiring on a very handsome pension. But the latest premium hike to $95,000—over seven times the original planned premium—just weren't part of his retirement plans, especially since he felt he no longer needed the insurance. When he ran the dilemma by his close friends, they agreed that the policy was no longer necessary. "If you continue to pay for it, you're not going to be able to do all the things you want in life," one of them said. "Walk away."

Being a prudent guy who always likes to consider his options, he decided to consult his CPA before letting his policy lapse. "Before you do anything," the professional said, "you really need to sit down and speak with a financial professional who specializes in life settlements. I'm not sure whether you'll get anything, but if you let it lapse, we know you're not going to get a dime."

When Donald and his CPA met with us, we knew right away that Donald was a candidate for a life settlement. In the four to seven years he probably had left, he certainly didn't need to be paying all that money for a policy he didn't need. But he also didn't need to leave money on the table. A bidding process finally resulted in a total gross offer of $315,000, close to twice the cash surrender value.

The recent premium hikes have proven too steep for a lot of people.

> The premium increased unexpectedly and I was no longer able to afford it. I was going to have to let the policy lapse.

Fortunately, if they no longer need their life insurance policy, they can trade in that expense and often wind up with enough cash to tick off an item or two on their bucket list.

Getting your money's worth

Even though we've been studying this whole situation for a while, as well as working up and reviewing financial plans for all our clients, we can't help being amazed at how many people continue to pay for costly insurance policies they don't need. And it's downright disconcerting when you consider the potential upside of selling those policies. In 2021, Americans who sold the life insurance policies they no longer needed instead of surrendering them averaged a solid 7.8 times more than the cash surrender value. That meant that American seniors pocked $660 million more than they would have had they just accepted what the life insurance carriers were offering.[9]

Alan Baxter is one of those who, rather than surrender the policy and wind up with less than he might have—or nothing at all—was able to profit significantly.

Alan, who has always had a passion for skiing—racing at Mount Hood in high school, working as a volunteer race coach after graduating college, and attending the winter Olympics whenever possible to see the downhill events—purchased a $2 million term policy 14 years ago to cover survivor needs for his children who were minors at that time. In the intervening years, his two sons, now in their mid-30s, had become successful professionals—one a fashion designer at Columbia Sportswear and the other a nurse at Providence Healthcare—and the end of the policy's 15-year term period was nearing.

Although Alan's first marriage ended in divorce, he is happily remarried to Kate, who has stuck by him despite challenges that could have destroyed flimsier relationships. In 2008, Alan's love for speed caught up with him—not on skis but behind the wheel of his beloved 1997 Porsche 930.

He had trailered his race car up to Portland International Raceway (PIR), just as he did several times each summer. As usual, he and his friend Roger had entered their cars into a race sanctioned by the Sports Car Club of America (SCCA), a nonprofit automobile club formed in 1944 that runs programs for amateur racing enthusiasts. This would be their first race since the track's recent and extensive renovation, which included repaving as well as widening turns four through seven and sharpening others to slow down racers before they entered the back straight.

Excited to try out the upgraded track, Alan pushed his mean machine hard. Although the course is almost perfectly flat, the track configuration includes a hard chicane at the end of the front straightaway. Coming into it with too much speed and not enough downshifting or braking action, he hit the new guardrail at over 150 mph. When he awoke at OHSU Spinal Center, he had no memory of the accident. Moments later, the doctor shared the news that Alan was now paralyzed from the waist down.

Although only 66, Alan, who is expected to live for just another four to seven more years, had to reevaluate many things, including his financial situation. When he expressed reservations about continuing to pay for or renewing his term policy since his kids, who were the only beneficiaries, were doing fine on their own, the accountant suggested that life settlement specialists review his policy. During the meeting, Alan was surprised to learn that rather than lapsing his term policy, which had no cash value, or paying more than $45,000 in annual premiums to convert the policy to a permanent policy, he could instead sell the term policy on the secondary market and recoup the $63,000 in cumulative premiums he had paid on the policy as well as additional funds to further enjoy his remaining years.

In the end, a bidding process and negotiated settlement offer brought in a total gross offer of $980,000, $917,000 more than he had paid in term premiums. Talk about creating value on an asset that so many people would assume was worthless!

An attractive environment to sell a policy

Now more than ever, the stars are aligned when it comes to selling a life insurance policy that is no longer needed or wanted. Let's look at the different factors causing this trend.

First and foremost, the low-interest-rate environment we have experienced over the past decade has led to a lot of money flowing into this market from institutional investors to buy policies as they seek higher returns than they can get from traditional fixed-income investments. Let's face it, not even institutions are happy with earning less than .5 percent in a savings account. One life settlement provider announced just a few years ago that it had secured $250 million from investors for policy purchases.[10]

Second, there is currently a great demand for policies and, therefore, more competition among buyers, resulting in what could be called a seller's market.

Third, buyers can borrow money at low interest rates to purchase policies and make future premium payments.

Fourth, life insurance policy values are an excellent non-correlating asset. This means they don't fluctuate with the ups and downs of the stock and real estate markets. The principal risk for investors is not stock market volatility or the safety of their investment. It's that the insured will live too long beyond life expectancy and make the policy purchase not economical.

Of course, an attractive selling environment doesn't necessarily mean that this is a good idea for you or your client. So how do you know whether you should consider a life settlement? That's next.

DEPOE BAY

BANDON DUNES

MERCEDES BENZ

HOTEL CASA DEL MAR

YANKEE STADIUM

SEATTLE

Chapter 2

YES, NO, OR MAYBE

SHOULD YOU OR YOUR CLIENT CONSIDER A LIFE SETTLEMENT?

The future depends on what you do today.
—*Mahatma Gandhi*

As we've already shared, a staggering 92 percent of life policies never pay out death benefits. Instead, they expire, lapse, or are surrendered before then. Had all those policyholders known about life settlements, they wouldn't have lost all those dollars. Research shows that, in hindsight, 90 percent of seniors would have considered a life insurance option had they known about it.[11]

Hindsight, as they say, is 20-20. And while it doesn't help the people who could have sold their life insurance policies, it can help you or your clients. Unfortunately, most people are not in the know. While life settlement transactions in the marketplace grew by 11 percent in 2020[12], with 3,241 people selling their life insurance policies for a combined total of more than $848 million, data in 2018 showed that 90 percent of consumers have no knowledge of life settlements.[13] We still believe that to be the case. Luckily, that's no longer the case for you. Larry's case illustrates how selling a life insurance policy can be a beneficial alternative to lapsing or surrendering it.

Playing with priorities

Larry and Liz Jacobs were household names in Depoe Bay, a town of fewer than 1,600 people located on the rugged Oregon Coast with the world's smallest navigable harbor. Picture-perfect especially when it's not raining (which is not very often), the seaside resort is best known for its whale watching. Larry and Liz were visionaries on that front, starting the first whale watching tour company in 1968.

Although one's chances for seeing whales year-round along the Oregon Coast are high, resident whales come close to shore to feed from June to mid-November. Depoe Bay is a hot spot for these giants of the sea looking for food at this time of year, which makes them very easy to spot.

During this same time period, Larry and Liz would barely have time to come up for air. Liz worked in the office taking reservations, selling tickets, and keeping the books organized while Larry and his best friend Otto led three to four daily tours. Otto, the Jacobs' 28-pound Corgi, loved the ocean. Despite his short stubby legs, he was always able to get up on the boat on his own and always looked "happy to be here" thanks to an infectious doggy smile. Smart, affectionate, and long, this working dog always needed a job to do. On the boat, his primary role was entertaining the paying guests while somehow receiving almost as much attention as the whales.

As the summer ended each year, the whales would slowly work their way back to Mexico just like many retired Oregon residents do. This timing worked out perfectly for Larry as it was also the off-season at the Bandon Dunes Golf Course, world famous for its Scottish-like grassy dunes that roll adjacent to the untamed and rugged Oregon coast. It also meant greens fees of $70 versus the steep $395 fare in the high season.

Sadly, when Liz died unexpectedly of health complications in 2012, Larry's spirit diminished as well. Suddenly, his visions of retirement had become permanently altered; his heart was no longer in his work. He ended up selling the business to a previous employee and not making as much money as he had hoped for.

Larry, now 88, had two life insurance policies that he originally purchased to help offset the inevitable estate taxes after he and Liz had both passed. Estate planning was an important topic for Larry and Liz as their goal was to transfer their combined assets to their two children in the most efficient way possible. Although not averse to paying their fair share of taxes, they just didn't want Uncle Sam to become their primary beneficiary. Back in 2012, the personal federal estate tax exemption amount was $5.12 million.[14] This meant that when someone died and the value of their estate was calculated, any amount more than $5.12 million was subject to the federal estate tax. To make matters worse, Oregon is one of a small handful of states that has a death tax as well.

Jump ahead to 2022 and the personal federal estate tax exemption has increased to $12.06 million[15], meaning that less than 1 percent of Americans currently have a federally taxable estate. That has changed the picture for Larry, who feels there is no longer a need for this coverage, which included one Universal Life policy for $1.2 million and another policy for $400,000.

My client took out a policy to cover future estate taxes, but today's estate taxes are no longer a concern. Selling his unneeded life insurance policy for cash today helped free up his retirement spending.

In addition, now that he was older, the premiums he had been paying for years would no longer buy the same amount of coverage. If he wanted to continue to fund his policies to age 100 at the same guaranteed level, he would have to pay more. A lot more.

Even though his life expectancy was less than five years, Larry was adamant about not paying the increased premiums the insurance company demanded. He preferred to use this money to visit Bandon Dunes during the peak season, on a scarce warm and sunny day, as he could still hit balls on their range.

Understanding Larry's wishes, his financial advisor in nearby Newport, Oregon, introduced him to the concept of a life settlement and referred him to our team. Working with multiple providers to negotiate settlement offers through an auction process, we were able to procure a gross offer of $975,000. This was not only 60 percent of Larry's total death benefit, but $842,000 more than his total cash surrender value of $133,000. He was thrilled to no longer pay his annual premiums of $133,000, and he even purchased a golf cart resembling a Mercedes Benz. Talk about golfing in style!

Life Settlement Basics

It's important to keep in mind that even when a life settlement may be an appropriate fit for a policy owner, they are complex transactions that require a team effort and a fair amount of time. Unlike purchasing a life insurance policy, which can sometimes take as little as a few weeks, trying to sell a policy and do it right takes an average of four to five months.

If a policy is about to lapse, there can be options to keep the policy in force while you weigh your options. Obviously, the biggest considerations when debating whether or not to sell will likely be how much you're spending on premiums and whether the policy is still necessary. When Jerry Weitzman did that very personal calculation, his answer was obvious.

Why keep paying for what you no longer need?

Jerry and his wife, Barbara, had recently celebrated their 65th wedding anniversary in style. They rented the Terrazza Lounge inside Hotel Casa Del Mar. This dynamic oceanfront hotel, located in the heart of Santa Monica, California, has a unique Mediterranean and beachy vibe they both appreciated. Jerry especially loved the live music featured every evening in the lounge, which partly explained why the location had become one of their favorite spots.

Jerry had played classical piano in his youth but gave it up upon entering his family business at the age of 20. Retirement 18 years ago allowed him to pick it back up and indulge his newly acquired passion for jazz piano. Even at the age of 88, he continues to impress his family and friends, as he did during the wedding anniversary bash when he took advantage of the Steinway inside the hotel lounge and pounded out tunes from his favorite pianist—the legendary Chick Corea, who embraced jazz fusion and then gave it a Latin flair. Every once in a while, Jerry wondered where his piano-playing could have taken him had he not taken a 50-year break. But, as always, family—and the family business—had come first.

Jerry's father had started a clothing manufacturing company in Los Angeles's garment district in 1924. Back then, this sub-neighborhood of downtown Los Angeles that straddled the border of Skid Row comprised 56 blocks. When Jerry's dad unexpectedly died of heart failure in 1974, Jerry assumed responsibility for keeping the family enterprise alive. He was only 40 at the time; however, having learned from the best in the business, Jerry had a quiet confidence that enabled him to forge ahead. His prudent decision to cut back the company's offerings and only produce two lines of silk pajamas—a budget and a high-end line—dramatically cut costs while increasing sales.

Jerry may have been the head honcho at work, but he was very aware that Barbara's genes ruled the roost at home, as they had three girls. Today, their daughters are all in the 60s, which is hard for him to believe. He also continues to face a very challenging time, often in disbelief that Barbara, a couple years his senior, recently passed away from ovarian cancer.

Back in 2001, Jerry had purchased two insurance policies when the federal estate tax exemption was $1 million, and the maximum estate tax rate was a whopping 55 percent.[16] Jerry's estate had grown to approximately $4 million by then, and he did not like the idea that all his estate above $1 million would be subject to estate tax upon his passing. As you know by now, since the time he purchased the policies, the estate tax exemption has increased to over $12 million, meaning that Jerry no longer needed insurance for his estate planning.

Jerry met with his insurance agent for a review of his policies. The first policy had a death benefit of $1,200,000, with a cash surrender value of $91,373. That didn't sound like a lot compared to the annual premiums of $72,852. The second policy had a death benefit of $400,000, a cash surrender value of $41,950, and annual premiums of $23,953.

Jerry's life expectancy was estimated to be approximately three years. On Jerry's behalf, the agent approached our team to investigate the possibilities of selling both of Jerry's policies. We were able to negotiate settlement offers that resulted in a gross offer of $975,000 for both policies. Jerry was delighted that the decision to sell his policies saves him the $96,175 a year it would have cost to maintain the policies. To top it off, in lieu of surrendering the policies as he originally planned, the gross offers resulted in more than 60 percent of the total death benefit.

WHO IS A LIFE SETTLEMENT FOR?

Life settlements will work great for some people, like Jerry, and not even be a consideration for others. So, let's review some rather common situations where a life settlement would be an option to consider:

- The need to replace lost income in case of the insured's death no longer exists as the kids may be out of the house and retirement may not be far away. The insurance is no longer needed, and the policy owner would like to terminate the policy and receive a lump sum cash payment.
- The premiums are no longer affordable because the carrier has significantly increased premiums. The policy owner no longer wants to pay additional premiums to keep the policy, which is no longer needed, in force.
- The long-term performance of the existing policy was poor, and the policy owner doesn't want to gamble on the outcome. (In this way, oddly, a life settlement becomes a risk management tool.)
- A convertible term policy is approaching the end of its specified term period (for example, 10 years). The policy owner can convert to a permanent policy, and through a life settlement, realize cash proceeds for an otherwise worthless asset. (We have found that many policy owners and their advisors are not aware that a convertible term policy is often a good candidate for a life settlement.)
- Policies owned by a charitable foundation are underperforming and should be replaced or terminated to accomplish the organization's goals.
- Family situations (such as divorce) occur that require modifications when it comes to insurance.
- Resources are required immediately for personal needs, such as a looming retirement, long-term care, or a family crisis.
- Funds to pay estate taxes are no longer required as the insured's estate will now fall within estate tax exemptions, rendering the life insurance unnecessary.

- Existing policies no longer meet the intentions of an irrevocable life insurance trust (ILIT).
- A highly compensated person in management retires and receives unneeded insurance through a deferred compensation arrangement.
- A business is sold, or changes take place within a buy-sell agreement (i.e., a partner leaves the company) that make the insurance no longer necessary.

My client was using a large portion of his retirement spending to fund an insurance policy that was originally intended to cover the business that was sold. Selling the policy dramatically improved his retirement liquidity.

In short, there are lots of reasons why you might want to ditch a life insurance policy that you no longer need instead of continuing to pay for it. There are even more options when it comes to spending the money you could receive for that policy. For some people, life settlements provide that expendable cash we all love so much. For others, a life settlement can be a lifeline, especially when life has dealt out an ugly hand.

FUNDS TO HELP WITH FAMILY EMERGENCIES

Reggie and Connie Johnson live in the suburbs of Greenville, North Carolina, where they raised their three children, who are all now successful in their careers. The city of just under 100,000 people—widely recognized as the thriving cultural, educational, economic, and medical hub for the state's eastern region—has been very good to them. Reggie is a successful home builder who creates one to two high-end, energy-efficient custom homes each year. He's a rare breed of builder who often becomes good friends his customers—even after the arduous building process is complete. He also likes to build rapport with his subcontractors, often bringing them hot coffee and warm muffins in the mornings. Just as importantly, he builds each home as if he and Connie were going to move into it.

Connie is the dean of students at East Carolina University's Brody School of Medicine. She is proud of the medical school's growing reputation and takes as much pride in her occupation as Reggie does building people's dream homes. She also shares her husband's passion for baseball.

Reggie has been a huge baseball fan since he was a youngster and still remembers the day in 1977, on his 18th birthday, when Reggie Jackson helped the New York Yankees win their first World Series in 15 years by hitting three home runs in a single game. Reggie had a tremendous amount of admiration for Mr. Jackson, later dubbed Mr. October, with whom he felt a personal connection considering that they shared the same first name and were both Black men.

Retirement had never been on Reggie's radar. He was too immersed in his work to even consider it. That single-minded focus would cost him. Thirteen years ago, at the age of 50, Reggie was advised by his doctor that he had hit that magic age when it was time to get a colonoscopy. Like many people, the thought of this procedure did not sound appealing, and he was just too busy to lose a day of work. Reggie waited another 10 years. Finally, at age 60, after Connie practically begged him, he finally got the rather simple outpatient procedure done. To his astonishment, the test results were not good.

"You have stage 3 colon cancer," the doctor announced in a very somber tone.

With a life expectancy that was suddenly only seven to eight years, it was time to reevaluate life's priorities. Fortunately, Reggie and Connie had accumulated a comfortable net worth so they could take an early retirement, while their son, Peter, who had been working with Reggie for the past eight years, was able to keep the family business alive.

Reggie owned a $300,000 convertible term policy that was originally obtained with the intention of replacing his income in the event of his passing, since Connie's income at that time was not sufficient to cover the family's cost of living. However, when Reggie and Connie met with Lynn, their financial advisor in Greenville, she informed them that the policy's conversion period was set to expire. As Reggie already owns an appropriate amount of permanent life insurance, they mutually determined that this term policy was no longer needed. Lynn then recommended a life settlement as a possible alternative to lapsing the policy and receiving nothing from the insurance company. They turned to our team.

We were able to negotiate a gross offer of $101,063. This unexpected windfall of "found money" staggered Reggie and Connie and reinforced the value of Lynn's professional guidance over all these years. The couple used these funds, over the following three seasons, to visit every single major league stadium in the MLB, including Yankee Stadium, where Reggie saw the enormous banners hanging in the great hall with pictures of past Yankee players including Babe Ruth, Joe DiMaggio, Mickey Mantle, Roger Maris, Yogi Berra, and of course Reggie Jackson.

Divorce changes just about everything

Just as family emergencies can yank the rug out from under you, so can a divorce. The one thing you're probably not thinking about as you struggle to claim your new life is the fact that you may very well have named your former spouse as a life insurance beneficiary. Luckily, Marc Dean's financial advisor had significant experience, so, when this restauranteur got into financial difficulty after his divorce, he had a place to turn.

The financial circumstances that prompted the downturn of Marc's restaurants surprised him just as much as—if not more—than the demise of his marriage. And Covid was no help. Marc and his former wife, Karen, had moved from Columbus, Ohio, to West Seattle, Washington, before having their two children, who are now both attending college. Over the years, Marc created three mid-range restaurants, each with a different theme and style. The ramen, seafood, and Italian eateries, which shared the same kind of trendy atmosphere along with a focus on friendly service and deliciously fresh ingredients, had been instant winners. For a while, he was on top of the world. Then, suddenly, he hit a bottom he never saw coming.

March of 2020 was the culmination of a perfect storm in Marc's life. The world's reality hit home when Covid-19 was declared a worldwide pandemic. That same week, the West Seattle Bridge was closed to traffic after workers observed growing cracks in its structure. A significant portion of his supplies and his customers traveled this main corridor to downtown Seattle. While the purveyors took the long way around to get to his place, most of the customers did not. Marc's 401(k) quickly became a 201(k) as his life savings in the stock market plummeted 34 percent. As if that wasn't enough, the following week, he learned something that would completely shatter his life: Karen was having an affair with a co-worker.

The idyllic life he thought he had only continued to implode from there. Friends and family members worried as they witnessed weight fall off him. He began experiencing abdominal pain, diarrhea, and fatigue. Was it the unbearable stress? As a believer in the mind/body connection, he assumed as much. Instead, Marc was diagnosed with Crohn's disease that led to intestinal cancer. His life expectancy was estimated at five years.

With the ugly reality of pandemic restrictions, staffing issues, supply chain problems, riots in the streets, a growing homelessness crisis, and his diagnosis, Marc reluctantly felt his only option was to permanently close his restaurants. Another dream splintered before his eyes.

Marc, now 55, not only had to confront health challenges, after his business closure and divorce he also had to come to terms with his finances. His 401(k) had been split in half yet again for obvious reasons. And he still had to make payments on the three $500,000 20-year term policies he had purchased

16 years ago as an income replacement for Karen and the kids, who were minors at the time but are currently both in high tech making great money. After meeting with his CPA, Marc was referred to our office to review his policies. He was delighted when he learned that we might be able to use a life settlement to convert his policies into much-needed cash while he was still alive.

Our Valmark life settlement team worked with multiple providers through its auction process to negotiate settlement offers resulting in a total gross offer of $304,800 for each policy. That's right, for each policy! The $914,400 Marc ended up with before commissions and expenses felt like free money to him. No, this would not extend his life or bring back the previous life he had created. But it did remove the tremendous financial stress Marc was under so he could live out his remaining years with significantly more peace of mind. He even had the ability to take his children and their partners to the Big Island of Hawaii.

Maybe not: Factors to consider

Life settlements can be a valuable source of liquidity for people planning to surrender their policies or allow them to lapse or for people whose life insurance needs have changed. But they are not for everyone.

While life settlements have proven to be quite profitable for those who sell their policies, it's important to be in the know regarding not just the benefits and rewards but the cons.

Here are some of the key factors you should consider when deciding whether to sell your life insurance policy:

- It's important to keep in mind that once you have transferred ownership of your policy to another entity or investor, your beneficiaries will no longer have a death benefit to collect upon your death.
- There will be tax consequences to a life settlement transaction as the proceeds from the sale of a policy may be subject to state or federal taxes. Before entering into a life settlement, check with a tax professional about the tax implications of any transaction you are considering.
- In addition to taxes, life settlements can have high transaction costs. These are paid out of the gross revenue from the sale of policies. It is important to have these fees disclosed in writing before you sign on with a life settlement broker.
- If you need cash and you would ideally like to maintain your coverage, you may be able to borrow against your policy or be eligible for accelerated death benefits. This feature enables a person with a long-term, catastrophic, or terminal illness to receive benefits on their policy while alive. Check with the company that issued your policy.
- Once your policy has been sold, your ability to purchase additional insurance in the future may be diminished or no longer available as your old policy will still be in force. This may affect your ability to get additional coverage.
- Even if you can get a new policy, you may have to pay higher premiums because of your age or changes in your health status.
- The life settlement industry is relatively new and may, sadly, target seniors who might be in poor health. The industry can also be prone to aggressive sales tactics and abuse. This makes it important to work with a reputable firm with a proven track record.

- Receiving a large payout could adversely affect one's eligibility for state or federal public assistance, such as Medicaid or other governmental programs. Before you proceed with a life settlement, be sure you fully understand the financial implications.
- It's important to consider your need for current income against the future financial needs of your survivors. You may have concluded that they do not need the proceeds from your insurance policy at this time. This situation, however, could change. Can you obtain the liquidity you may want from other sources?
- Section 1035 of the Internal Revenue Code allows you to exchange an insurance policy that you own for a new life insurance policy insuring the same person without paying tax on the investment gains earned on your original contract. A "1035 exchange" to a new, potentially less expensive policy can be a beneficial alternative.

I needed money to pay for long-term care costs, and my retirement assets were getting low.

It's worth repeating: Knowing all your options as you consider implementing major changes to an existing policy is critical. A life settlement may or may not be the best alternative for you, so you should be aware of all your alternatives before making up your mind. A life insurance policy is a valuable asset, so it's imperative to consider all the factors listed above before deciding to sell a policy.

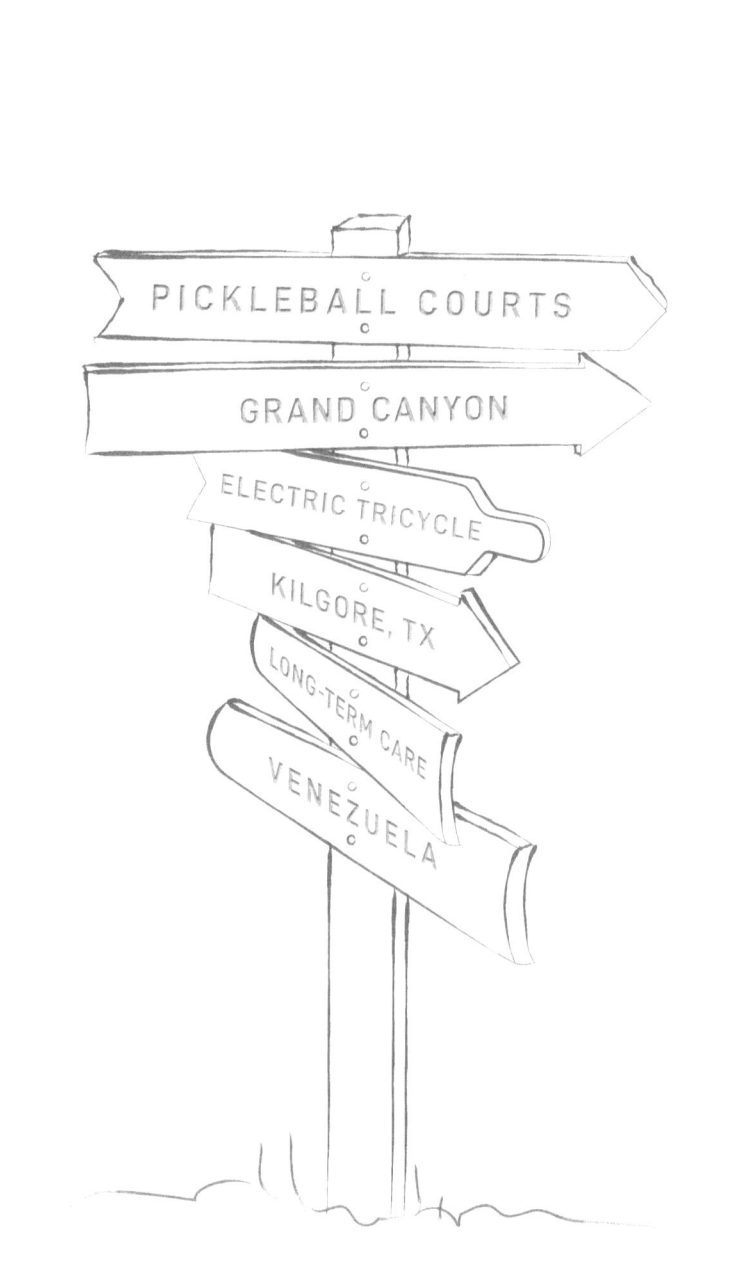

- PICKLEBALL COURTS
- GRAND CANYON
- ELECTRIC TRICYCLE
- KILGORE, TX
- LONG-TERM CARE
- VENEZUELA

Chapter 3

NOT AN ALL-OR-NOTHING PROPOSITION

Cashing In on Part of Your Life Insurance

*Life is like riding a bicycle.
To keep your balance, you must keep moving.*
—*Albert Einstein*

Wouldn't life be simple if everything was a black-and-white, yes-or-no proposition? Of course, as we all know by now, that's not the way things are. And frankly, all those shades of gray make things a lot more interesting. But competing interests also make our lives more challenging. Fortunately, when it comes to life settlements, you don't have to decide to either sell, sell, sell or hold, hold, hold. You can do both.

Consider this example of a hypothetical couple entering retirement who no longer have a need for life insurance. Let's say that at age 55, the husband purchased a life insurance policy with a $2 million death benefit. Twenty years later at the age of 75, his children are grown up and financially successful. He has a granddaughter with a disability and his intentions are to leave a $500,000 bequest to her. Rather than receive a lump sum cash payment for selling the entire policy, he could sell $1.5 million of the policy, and in place of receiving compensation for the entire portion of the policy, he retains $500,000 of the death benefit and no longer has to make another premium payment. His granddaughter will receive $500,000 upon his passing. And like all life insurance policies, she will receive this in a tax-free manner.

Don't you love that?

But why consider a hypothetical story when we can talk about real ones?

Making an informed decision

Glen and Marcia Barrett relocated to Tucson, Arizona, shortly after retiring. Glen had a successful 40-year career as an orthopedic surgeon in Chicago. His specialty was radiofrequency ablation (RFA), a procedure used to treat pain in one's lower back. This relatively simple outpatient technique uses a needle electrode that sends electrical currents to the pinched nerves in one's joints. The electrical currents create heat that damages the nerve so it can no longer send pain signals to the brain. Glen had always received great satisfaction witnessing his patients enter his office with debilitating discomfort and then leave pain-free just an hour later.

The Barrett's palm-tree-lined retirement community looks and functions like a resort. The couple enjoys playing pickleball on one of the tennis courts that was recently converted to meet the demand of this fast-growing sport, followed by a swim in one of the three pools. Most evenings are spent in their backyard with friends as they watch the sunset, a Manhattan in hand.

Most of the community's residents, who largely hail from the Midwest as well as Canada, return to their hometowns when the sweltering heat sets in each May. Glen and Marcia own one home and make the best of the hot summers. Sadly, this is not by choice as they lost a significant portion of their wealth after investing Glen's entire 401(k) into a medical device startup that later declared bankruptcy. Even though they have not been able to maintain the lifestyle that they were accustomed to, their marriage has fortunately stayed strong.

Glen recently celebrated his 74th birthday. He had two different term insurance policies with a total death benefit of $5 million. The $3 million policy needed to be converted into a permanent policy if it were to remain in force. His second policy had a death benefit of $2 million; however, this policy was not convertible. When referred to our practice, Glen shared with us that he could no longer afford making the steep premium payments of $92,000 for the $3 million policy and $46,535 for the $2 million policy.

After learning that his life expectancy was estimated to be between seven and nine years, we felt confident that we would receive multiple offers for his policies, which would potentially increase the value we could get for them.

We are fortunate to have access to Valmark's Policy Management Company™(PMC), which is unique to the insurance industry. We run each and every policy through this system, regardless of whether we are ensuring that a client's life insurance policy is being managed properly or whether someone is considering a potential life settlement. This enables our team and our clients to make an informed decision they're comfortable with.

The PMC monitors our client's policies. This is imperative as even the simplest life insurance policies, which are customized for each individual client, are intricate and multi-faceted. Life insurance policies have many moving parts that include everything from structuring the premium, varied underwriting classifications, and unique contractual provisions. These policies are based on a promise to deliver a payment in 20 to 40 years' time. Like any product purchased to last for an extended period of time, however, things can go awry if no one is keeping an eye on it. Life insurance is no exception. If your policy is not being properly supervised, many things can happen during the policy's lifetime that can change or void the original expectations.

To help protect our policy owners against any potential derailments, the Policy Management Company™ provides an annual audit of each policy. This hands-on supervision includes:

- Confirming that premiums are always paid
- Evaluating policy performance
- Access to all policy information in one centralized location
- Confidence that your insurance needs are always covered
- Automated trust administration and documented policy performance
- Ongoing service by a trusted third party

After running both of Glen's policies through the PMC, Glen and Marcia decided to sell $2 million of Glen's $3 million convertible policy, which netted a gross payment of $475,000. This felt like free money to them since before meeting us they were ready to walk away from this policy with nothing. To top it off, we later received an offer of $174,300 for Glen's $2 million policy. As a result, Glen and Marcia are now able to pay the premiums on the remaining $1 million death benefit using the gross proceeds from the sale. Glen was relieved to know he could afford to maintain some coverage for Marcia's survivorship needs while improving their retirement lifestyle. They plan to use a chunk of the proceeds to take a six-week trip to Europe this summer, which will include a Viking cruise on the Rhine River. Plans for the following summer already include the Danube.

> The premiums on my 88-year-old client quadrupled and he was unable to afford it. I recommended a life settlement and got an offer of 30 percent of the death benefit.

The takeaway here is that there's often considerable flexibility in how policies can be marketed and sold. We were able to help structure this life settlement where $4 million of the $5 million of face amount was sold on the open market, enabling our clients to pay for the premiums of the remaining $1 million policy while significantly increasing their retirement cash flow. Glenn and Marcia are looking forward to escaping the summer heat of Arizona.

Making the most of your resources

Of course, Arizona isn't the only place that bakes during the summer. Texas, which is where Belle Morrison lives, can register plenty of high heat as well. Belle grew up in the 1930s in Kilgore, Texas. There was only one reason her dad moved the family to this remote town located in the eastern part of the state between Dallas and Shreveport, Louisiana. It was not chicken-fried steak. It was liquid gold. Kilgore's fortunes changed dramatically in 1930, when a friend of Belle's father, Columbus Joiner, struck oil near the neighboring town of Henderson. Seemingly overnight, Kilgore was transformed from a small farming town on the decline into a bustling boomtown.

In high school, Belle tried out and was accepted onto the respected Kilgore Rangerettes in their second year after being formed. When Belle wasn't performing with the precision dance team that's still entertaining people today, she was reading romance novels. So, it was no surprise to anyone who knew her when she eventually became a successful romance novelist. Her books won numerous literary awards, provided her with a great feeling of gratification, and contributed a significant supplement to her family's income.

Today, Belle is 89 years young and is a firm believer that graying means playing. She likes to say she traded her rocking chair in for an electric tricycle. Her fat-tire bike has 750 watts, which enables her to smoothly accelerate to the corner market and back. Even after her husband Frank passed away several years ago, a grieving Belle managed to retain her contagiously positive spirit, which she shares with her four grandchildren and two great-grandkids.

Although she has a sizeable net worth, her nest egg diminished significantly over the six years that Frank needed at-home health care before eventually being located into a costly memory care center. No one had ever informed Frank and Belle of long-term care insurance when they were both younger and healthy. Knowing how much this had cost them, Belle decided to have a professional look over her investments as well as provide advice on her life insurance policies, including one policy held by the family trust with a $6 million death benefit.

Belle was referred to an independent financial advisor by a close friend she respects. The advisor determined that the 89-year-old needed additional liquidity to pay the premiums on this large universal life policy with a cash surrender value of approximately $93,000. It was important to Belle that the prearranged inheritance for her family and charities remain intact.

We put up her policy for auction and negotiated the highest settlement bid with a gross offer of $1.565 million. This amount was 26 percent of the policy's death benefit and 16 times the cash surrender value. Rather than continue to make premium payments that were a financial stretch for Belle, she collected this seven-figure unexpected inflow. Her remaining policy will eventually provide a tax-free payout to her loved ones and local nonprofits that are near and dear to her heart.

> *My client was spending down her retirement quickly, and soon would have to sell everything to qualify for Medicaid. Selling her unneeded policy provided additional funds to cover increasing retirement and long-term care expenses.*

GETTING WHAT YOU DESERVE

According to a recent GAO study, life settlements deliver more than four times the surrender value to seniors.[17] So, a life settlement can often be an advantageous alternative to lapsing or surrendering a life insurance policy, especially since providers have more institutional money available to bid on policies than they previously had.

Of course, not all of us are lucky enough to have multiple policies like Belle—or even a family trust. For a lot of us, times have just gotten hard. That was certainly the case for Hugh Sawyer.

As a child, he would always flip through the pages of his parents' National Geographic magazines and lust after the idea of traveling to exotic places such as Africa and South America. After graduating from Cal Poly San Luis Obispo, located in California's Central Coast, Hugh, like so many graduates, had absolutely no idea what he wanted to do in life. Applying to the Peace Corps felt like a natural next move and certainly made more sense for him than joining the armed forces. It was no surprise to his family and friends that he was quickly accepted. Within three months, Hugh found himself stationed in Ciudad Bolívar, the capital of Venezuela's southeastern Bolívar state. His mission for the next two years would be to help construct a waterpipe below the Angostura suspension bridge to make safe drinking water more accessible to the smaller villages located outside of the city.

Hugh quickly fell in love with the kind people, the majestic mountain scenery, and the local cuisine. His two-year stint flew by, and he matured in ways even his parents couldn't have imagined. He returned to the United States a confident young man who was so much more comfortable in his skin. Once home, it didn't take him long to realize how much he missed South American culture.

How could I get paid to return to Venezuela? he wondered. Before long, Hugh decided to start an adventure tour operating company. With a loan from his parents that he proudly paid back within one year, his business plan actually worked. Jump ahead five years and Hugh had seven full-time staff and had created a reputation among well-to-do baby boomers who missed the adventure of their youth and were willing to pay a premium for an organized tour that was about immersion into the native culture rather than 1,500-thread-count Egyptian cotton sheets at the Ritz Carlton. Hugh was making a handsome living and felt he had won the lottery as his occupation did not entail a desk job or a suit and tie like so many of his friends back in the states.

Fast-forward to February of 2020, when Hugh celebrated his 59th birthday. He still loved his work so much that retirement wasn't on his radar, although he chuckled to himself in disbelief that he was of the age to access his IRAs without penalty. *Where did the time go?* Just weeks after his birthday, Hugh's world as well as the rest of the world changed in ways no one could fathom. He had never heard of the terms "coronavirus" or "Covid," but this global pandemic quickly became a reality. The stock market precipitously dropped and so did his tour company's months of booked reservations. He held on for months, hoping the virus would subside and international borders would open back up. Then the delta variant took hold. By the time the omicron variant appeared, Hugh's business had dried up to nothing. The bureaucracy of Venezuela along with their incredibly rampant inflation of 2,959 percent in 2020[18] certainly did not help matters. (And we thought the US 40-year-high inflation rate of 8.6 percent[19] was a lot! Think again.) Hugh had no choice but to close his business. As a result, he was forced to file bankruptcy to discharge business loans for which he was personally responsible.

Hugh had a $1 million term life insurance policy, which needed to be converted within the next several months. However, he could not afford to pay the annual premium of $17,800 for a permanent policy and, like all term policies, his existing policy had no cash value. He felt he had no choice but to surrender his policy and walk away with nothing. That was, until his financial advisor referred him to our practice. We ran an analysis on all the options Hugh had so he could make an informed decision he was comfortable with. Sadly, we learned his life expectancy was estimated to be less than six years due to being diagnosed, several years earlier, with chronic lower respiratory disease (CLRD). This condition, which affects the lungs, is considered to be the fourth-leading cause of death in the United States.

After working with multiple providers, we were able to obtain an offer of $490,000 for Hugh's $1 million policy. Although this news brought significant relief to Hugh and would make his remaining years significantly less stressful on the financial front, it was important for him to leave a legacy for his girlfriend of many years. So, we shared with Hugh the idea of retaining $250,000 of his insurance policy and selling $750,000. He received a gross offer of $295,000 plus reimbursement of the first quarter's premium. This offer was 39 percent of the total death benefit. Hugh's life settlement enabled him to retain part of his insurance, thereby leaving a legacy for his loved one, while enjoying his remaining years comfortably and with dignity.

Hugh's situation, and with Glen's, Marcia's, and Belle's situations, are just some of the many client scenarios in which a life settlement can provide an attractive alternative to lapsing or surrendering part of a policy or all of it.

How you decide to structure your life settlement is up to you. Getting you that life settlement is our job. That's not the easiest, as you'll see in the next chapter. But when it works, wow! What a gift!

- GUANAJUATO, MX
- WORLD HERITAGE SITE
- SURFING
- DRIGGS, ID
- AUCTION

Chapter 4

HOW IT WORKS

The Process Behind Obtaining a Life Settlement

Change is not an event, it's a process.
—Cheryl James

Is a life settlement starting to sound like it might make sense for you or your client? American management consultant and author W. Edwards Deming once said, "If you do not know how to ask the right question, you discover nothing." Of course, since you can't actually talk to us right now (unless you pick up the phone, which you're more than welcome to do), we've tried to anticipate the questions you might have, starting with how this whole process works, what you can expect, and how you would go about evaluating this possibility and making a solid financial choice for yourself or your client.

MAKING A GOOD BUSINESS DECISION

As we saw in the last chapter, Glen, Marcia, Belle, and Hugh all decided to sell their life insurance policies based on information garnered from a review of their personal finances. But that wasn't the only decision that would lead to a boost of their financial reserves. They also opted to work with us. And while this last statement sounds ridiculously self-serving, that move made a monstruous difference.

1 EVALUATE
2 MARKET
3 AUCTION
4 NEGOTIATE
5 CLOSING

For those considering selling an insurance policy, having a broker who works on their behalf has everything to do with whether they obtain the highest price for their policy. As client advocates, we market the insurance policy to the majority of the leading life settlement providers (those organizations bidding on policies), launch a formal auction, and negotiate offers with the objective of getting the highest fair market value.

Many life settlement providers will show interest in handling viable policies that are purchasable. However, it is critical to know that their mission is to look after their investors buying the policy and not you, the policy owner. As a result, their goal is to pay as little as possible for your policy. Our goal is to eliminate the possibility of a single provider making a low-ball offer. Let's look how our auction process is designed to create competition that drives providers to pay top dollar for your policy.

OUR COMPETITIVE PROCESS

We have long-term relationships with most of the industry's top life settlement providers. Some are names with which you may be familiar, while others are exclusive to our broker network. We feel it's imperative to shop every policy to every one of these providers in the marketplace. Although we have gained historical insight into pricing over the years, to better help our clients, our team has created software that helps us estimate the potential value of a policy so that, when we receive an offer, we know if it is even in the ballpark.

Whenever we receive an offer, our system keeps the other bidders in the loop. These automatic notifications to providers on the bids we have received encourage the various would-be buyers to stay active in the bidding process. Naturally, keeping other providers in the process intensifies the competition and helps drive up the price until the top dollar is attained. In almost all cases, the winning provider is willing to pay significantly more for the policy than their initial low offer.

During the bidding process, we feel it's crucial that all providers play on the same level playing field and that our clients looking to sell their policy are receiving the highest offer possible. To accomplish this, our team at Valmark uses a formal written bid process that is unique in the industry and that provides uniquely profitable results.

To help describe how lucrative this auction process can be, let's look at a recent case where the final settlement bid increased by 226 percent.

The power of an auction

Alfredo Gonzales, better known as Alf in his community, was born and raised in Guanajuato City in the mountains of central Mexico. This picture-perfect town resembles a Hollywood set with houses in every imaginable color that plunge down the hills. The sinuous cobblestone streets lead to quaint plazas, historic cathedrals, and colonial-era mansions. So it's no surprise that Guanajuato is a World Heritage site. At the age of 18, Alf and his parents moved to Huntington Beach, California. After 45 years in this scenic beach town, Alf has become renowned for his generosity as he continues to dedicate significant free time to work with at-risk youth. More recently, he's also been able to focus on another favorite pastime.

For 23 years, Alf worked at the nearby Boeing facility. He was part of an engineering team that created the Delta III and Delta IV rockets, as well as components of the International Space Station. When Boeing shut this plant in 2020, Alf decided it was an opportune time to retire. He was eager to surf the waves on dawn patrol each morning instead of only being able to hit the beach after work and on the weekends. His friends refer to him as "old school" as he surfs a vintage 1967 Greg Noll longboard. Alf always responds with a grin: "Old school is better than no school."

Sadly, two years into his retirement, Alf began dealing with unexpected health ailments. He had a life insurance policy that he determined he no longer wanted or needed. After we presented him with the four viable options for his policy, which as you may remember are surrendering the policy, reducing the death benefit, paying the increased premiums, or selling the policy, he made an informed decision to have us sell his policy. This kicked off the auction process.

Our team got Alf's policy into the hands of 13 prominent life settlement providers from around the country. Initial offers, ranging from $100,000 to $250,000, hit quickly. At this point, many brokers would have accepted the highest offer and Alf would have been delighted to receive a quarter of a million dollars for a policy he no longer wanted. However, we were only getting started. We sent the highest offer from round one back to all the providers with the intention of procuring boosted offers. Our tactic worked. By the time the auction process ended in round 28, the final offer was 715 percent higher than the initial bid on his policy. Alf received a gross offer that had skyrocketed to $815,000!

| | \multicolumn{14}{c|}{Auction Rounds} |
	1	2	3	4	5	6	7	8	9	10	11	12	13	14
Bidder 1	$910,000	$960,000	$1,012,500											
Bidder 2	$900,000	$1,000,000	$1,050,000	$1,075,000	$1,086,000	$1,125,000								
Bidder 3	$990,000				$1,100,000	$1,150,000								
Bidder 4	$900,000	$966,600	$1,021,600	$1,076,000	$1,086,000	$1,100,000	$1,150,000	$1,200,000	$1,270,000	$1,270,000	$1,250,000	$1,250,000	$1,270,000	$1,280,000
Bidder 5	$900,000	$1,002,500	$1,002,500	$1,065,000	$1,076,000	$1,126,000	$1,126,000	$1,170,000	$1,160,000	$1,200,000	$1,220,000	$1,260,000	$1,270,000	$1,270,000
Bidder 6	$925,000	$975,000	$1,020,000	$1,060,000	$1,100,000	$1,100,000	$1,145,000		$1,170,000	$1,270,000	$1,250,000	$1,260,000	$1,270,000	
Bidder 7	$920,000	$980,000	$1,012,500	$1,060,000	$1,086,000	$1,136,000								
Bidder 8	$950,000	$950,000	$1,002,500	$1,060,000	$1,086,000									
Bidder 9	$960,000													
9 Bidders	No offers													

The gross offer listed in this chart will be reduced by commissions and expenses related to the sale. Each client's experience varies, and there is no guarantee that a life settlement will generate an offer greater than the current cash surrender value. In such cases, the client can always surrender their policy to the carrier if the coverage is no longer needed. This table is intended for visual illustration and for informational purposes only and should not be construed as a specific example of any client's experience.

This notable result emphasizes the importance of having a formal written bid process, which allows our clients to feel confident that they are receiving the fair market value for their policy or policies.

THE LIFE SETTLEMENT TIMELINE

By introducing the policy to multiple carriers, the competitive nature of the auction has often helped client experience a rising bid process that ultimately creates value for the client. In some cases, clients have experienced up to 187% increase from the original offer. As you might imagine, a considerable amount of effort is involved in achieving such results from the sale of a policy. It also takes a well-oiled and coordinated process to establish connection to multiple carriers and field their independent bids to complete the transaction. However, each and every auction is unique and the experience of one or even many auctions can vary over time. Like any industry, the appetite for certain business lines may change with the market conditions. Past performance of auction processes should not be relied upon as an expectation for future auction experiences. While there is no guarantee of a successful auction, the process always culminates with the customer having the final review and acceptance or rejection of the final auction result.

Life settlements don't just happen. And, as you will see, they sure don't happen overnight. The timeline below illustrates the sequence and time frames required to make the sale of your policy a smooth process.

- **STEP 1 (three days) – A Life Settlement Evaluation™:** This involves our team procuring information to evaluate your health and estimate your life expectancy. We also

get detailed information on the policy or policies you are contemplating putting up for sale.
- **STEP 2 (how long this takes depends on you) – Life Settlement Formal Application:** Once your case is pre-qualified, it's time to complete the paperwork to get the ball rolling. This includes filling out HIPAA authorizations and providing us with medical contacts so our underwriting team can obtain your medical records, which, of course, are kept confidential.
- **STEP 3 (one-two months) – Preparing for Market:** In this step, we obtain your medical records and life expectancy report. This enables us to create a Policy Appraisal Report™, which will give us a preliminary estimate on what we feel the fair market value of your policy will be. Once that's in place, we're ready to go to market.
- **STEP 4 (one month) – Marketing the Policy:** It's now time to send your well-prepared and packaged policy information to the numerous life settlement providers. We begin to collect their initial offers.
- **Step 5 (one-two months) – The Formal Auction Process:** As providers bid for your policy, our automatic notifications back to the providers on the bids we receive encourages them to stay active in the bidding process and helps drive up the price. To obtain the highest offer, there are often numerous rounds in the bidding process. You decide which bid, if any, you want to accept. The experience, professionalism, reputation, and the closing time of the provider should be factored in, so the highest price may not always be the best offer. After we review all offers and the offer is accepted by all parties, a formal settlement offer letter is signed.

How it Works

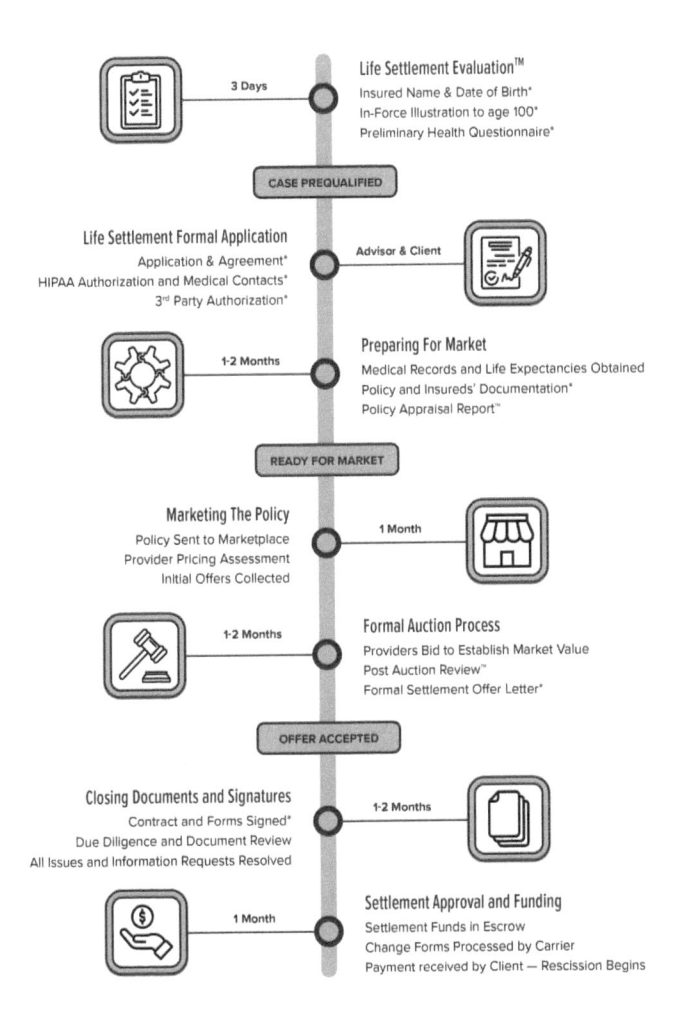

Life Settlement Evaluation™ — 3 Days
- Insured Name & Date of Birth*
- In-Force Illustration to age 100*
- Preliminary Health Questionnaire*

CASE PREQUALIFIED

Life Settlement Formal Application — Advisor & Client
- Application & Agreement*
- HIPAA Authorization and Medical Contacts*
- 3rd Party Authorization*

Preparing For Market — 1-2 Months
- Medical Records and Life Expectancies Obtained
- Policy and Insureds' Documentation*
- Policy Appraisal Report™

READY FOR MARKET

Marketing The Policy — 1 Month
- Policy Sent to Marketplace
- Provider Pricing Assessment
- Initial Offers Collected

Formal Auction Process — 1-2 Months
- Providers Bid to Establish Market Value
- Post Auction Review™
- Formal Settlement Offer Letter*

OFFER ACCEPTED

Closing Documents and Signatures — 1-2 Months
- Contract and Forms Signed*
- Due Diligence and Document Review
- All Issues and Information Requests Resolved

Settlement Approval and Funding — 1 Month
- Settlement Funds in Escrow
- Change Forms Processed by Carrier
- Payment received by Client — Rescission Begins

- **Step 6 (one-two months) – Closing Documents:** Now that the offer has been accepted, it's time to sign the contracts. All documents are reviewed and any additional requests for information are answered. Then comes the reward for all this work—the close!

- **Step 7 (one month) – Settlement Approval and Funding:** The settlement funds are held in escrow while the forms are updated at the life insurance company, and we await full payment from the provider. When the transaction is complete, the buyer—or life settlement provider—becomes the new owner of the life insurance policy, pays future premiums, and collects the death benefit when the insured dies. And you get to use the proceeds of the sale any way you want. Wahoo!

This process can really pay off

Whenever something would take an unexpectedly long time, one of our friends used to say, "A guy could eat a pomegranate." When it comes to life settlements, we're talking about cases of pomegranates. But the wait, as trying as it may be, can wind up being positively worthwhile.

Let's look at another real-life example of a client who benefited greatly from the advantages of using that professional auction process. Daniel Ferguson is a 55-year-old business owner from Driggs, Idaho. Thirteen years ago, he purchased a $1.75 million term policy after buying a substantial interest in a successful local manufacturing business. The majority owner of the company, who had sold a portion of his shares to Daniel, insisted on taking out a life insurance policy on his new, younger business partner. This would provide financial security in case something happened to Daniel. In the event of Daniel's passing, 40 percent of the death benefit was assigned to the seller to cover Daniel's loan and the remainder was assigned to Daniel's wife, Juliane.

A few years into the partnership, Daniel learned he had cancer. His doctor informed him his life expectancy was estimated to be two to three years. No couple can ever prepare for such shocking news. To make matters worse, the experimental medical procedures Daniel decided to undergo were not accepted by his health insurance company. The Fergusons needed cash and they needed it immediately to defray the excessive medical expenses and other bills that seemed to bombard them daily. After consulting his accountant, Daniel was referred to our group to review his policy. We shared the four options Daniel had regarding his policy. His face lit up when he learned that he did not have to wait to die to benefit from at least part of his death benefit.

After he and Juliane decided that selling the policy was their most favorable option, we jump-started the auction process.

Six rounds of bidding later, we were eager to share that the highest gross offer we had received was $1.28 million. This would provide tremendous peace of mind for the couple as it would cover their recent debt and enable them to travel as well as to save funds for Juliane's future, which was a priority for Daniel.

It turned out that in the interim, Daniel had consulted with a single provider about attaining an offer for his policy. This is certainly a less-traveled route to selling a policy, and one that is not likely to generate the best offer for the seller as there is no auction process. The fact that the single provider only offered Daniel $1.1 million for his policy showed him (and reinforced for our team) the advantages of our auction process, which encourages multiple providers to take part. The extra $180,000 we obtained for him—16 percent more than he would have received—is nothing to sneeze at.

In review, as brokers, we have a fiduciary responsibility to you, the seller of the policy, as opposed to life settlement providers that have a fiduciary duty to the third-party companies buying your life insurance policy. Their goal is to pay a minimal amount to purchase the policy. Our goal is to ensure you receive the highest price. This certainly made a big difference for Daniel and Juliane.

Determining Policy Fair Market Value

You're probably wondering how in the world companies determine a fair price for your policy. It all revolves around an important point that we've discussed before but that's worth repeating. Once a policy is sold, the seller receives a cash payment, and the buyers begin paying all the premiums moving forward until the insured dies. Then, and only then, do the new owners of the policy receive the death benefit.

Let's look at the three key factors related to this fact and the impact each of them has on determining the value of a policy.

1. The death benefit
2. The cost of future premiums
3. The life expectancy of the insured

The providers who purchase life insurance policies are understandably looking to profit from such a transaction. The higher the death benefit, the lower the premiums, and the shorter the life expectancy, the greater their enthusiasm. Providers are willing to pay a higher amount for such a policy since they're likely to reap more money sooner. Conversely, the higher the premiums that must be paid to keep the policy in force and the longer they must wait to receive the death benefit, the smaller the profit. Logically, to make this second scenario a smart investment, they have to offer a reduced amount.

Every life insurance policy is unique and has its own variables. The good news is the death benefit is always known and most policies have an annual premium that can be determined within a reasonable probability. The biggest uncertainty and risk for the buyers/investors is the remaining life of the insured. Although they consider one's age, gender, lifestyle, and overall health, predicting how long any one individual will live is uncertain. Of course, their bad news on that front is the seller's cause for celebration.

While it can be unsettling for some people to know that their life expectancy and health are being evaluated in terms of dollars and cents, that's countered by some seriously good news. A life settlement will put more money in your bank account than letting your unwanted policy simply lapse.

Just how much will your fun coupons grow by? Clearly, that depends a lot on the three elements we've just discussed. But the ultimate offer you receive for your life insurance policy can also have a whole lot to do with who is advocating for you. That's next.

- SEAL BEACH
- LIBRARY
- BROADWAY
- SARATOGA SPRINGS
- PICKLE BALL
- WHITEFISH

Chapter 5

CHOOSING WHOM YOU WORK WITH

The Right Professional Can Make All the Difference

Excellence is a continuous process and not an accident.
—*A.P.J. Abdul Kalam, former president of India*

Before we go any further, let's address the elephant in the room. While life settlements may potentially yield a small or large financial bonanza, which we love, they can usually only be put into play when you or your client are of a certain age and with a defined and somewhat limited life expectancy. That's not the easiest thing to think about or talk about. So, if you're going to take the plunge on that front, you want to make sure of two things:

- You feel comfortable with the person you've chosen to work with
- That person has clearly defined processes in place designed to deliver the biggest bang for your buck.

For starters, that means that you want to work with someone who has your financial interest at heart rather than the buyer's. We'll talk more about that in the next chapter. For now, we want to show you what a difference selecting the right person to work with can make.

Wesley and Janice Nguyen live in Garden Grove, California, where Wesley spent much of his career as the CFO of a large manufacturing company that fabricates parts for the aerospace and defense industries. He loved his work but was also happy to retire four years ago at the age of 69.

Today, the couple enjoys taking their grandchildren to Seal Beach every Sunday for ice cream when they're not visiting their cottage in Big Bear Lake. Although they no longer ski at the nearby resort, they enjoy the more temperate summer climate at 6,700 feet.

Wesley purchased a $2.1 million insurance policy on his life back when he was the CFO. One evening, Wesley saw a television commercial on life settlements. He had never heard about the concept of selling one's policy, so the ad sparked his interest as he no longer needed the coverage and was not very keen to continue paying the $114,600 annual premium. He tried to sell his policy to the ad's direct-to-consumer buyer and received an offer of $210,000. While this offer was more than twice the value of his current $100,000 cash value, his gut told him he had been low-balled. Could he do better? To find out, Wesley began doing some additional research and approached our office to obtain a second opinion. Wesley was understandably fee-concious and inquired about the potential offer he might anticipate along with the costs involved in such a transaction. After describing our auction process and our estimate of what we felt the value of his policy was, he decided to go with us instead of accepting the offer he had received.

Each life settlement case is distinct. Wesley's life expectancy ranged from 87 to 127 months, which is longer than most in the life settlement world. Even so, once our auction process had been completed, we wrote a check to Wesley for $409,000. This amount was after our fee was taken off the top and almost twice his previous offer.

I owned a large policy to cover my business, but now that I have retired, I don't need it anymore.

NOT A CASE OF ONE AND DONE

As you now know full well from Wesley's story and those in the last chapter, having a robust auction process makes a world of difference when it comes to securing a higher life settlement offer. But that's not the only way that life settlements materialize, especially since sometimes there's just a single offer.

With the right professional, however, that single offer doesn't have to be the final answer. Our Valmark team managed to negotiate a 25 percent higher price for a client than the original offer despite only getting one bid.

What a difference a year can make

Truth be told, even when you've aligned yourself with the best in the business, selling a life insurance policy doesn't always work the first time around. So, you want to work with a team with the persistence to try, try, try again—one for whom failure is not an option.

That's what Judith Wakefield did. At the age of 83, her life's passion is still centered around books. She retired as a librarian after a four-decade career. Since her husband passed away, she has been volunteering her time at the library part-time. What most people don't know about her is that she's a closet novelist—literally. Not only does she not tell a lot of people about her pastime, but she has half a dozen manuscripts that she's written squirreled away on the floor of her linen closet. She likes to say with a grin: "A reader lives a thousand lives before she dies. That's even more true for the writer who creates those characters."

When you think librarian, the words *riches* or *wealth* probably don't come to mind. However, Judith's late husband, Robert, had been a successful executive of a Fortune 100 company. Years before, he had purchased a $3.75 million policy on Judith's life as he always believed in the powerful leverage life insurance provides. The challenge Judith faced was that her policy was upside down. You see, her cash surrender value was $124,000 but she had a loan on this policy for $258,000. Since the annual premium was just making matters worse, her plan was to let the policy lapse and walk away from it, so that she would only have to contend with the loan payments. That is, until her attorney referred her to us.

With Judith's life expectancy between four and six years, we were a bit surprised when we didn't receive a single offer after attempting the sell her policy. It was then that we channeled Ryan Holiday and his powerful quote: "Genius often really is just persistence in disguise." After letting the dust settle for a year, we decided to try selling Judith's life insurance policy again. This time, our auction process went to 13 rounds. Talk about patience paying off! If only you could have seen Judith's face when we informed her that we had negotiated a gross offer of $1.125 million—30 percent of her face amount. That cash inflow brought her significant joy and financial peace of mind. Secretly, we hope she uses some of this money to get one or more of her manuscripts professionally edited and published.

EARLY BEGINNINGS

Before we continue to explore how the person or team you choose to work with will impact how your life settlement turns out, let's answer that one question I know all you enquiring minds want to know.

How did this all get started?

This life settlement business dates back to 1911 when a landmark decision was made by the U.S. Supreme Court in the case of *Grigsby v. Russell*.[20] This ruling gave life insurance policyowners the rights to transfer ownership of their life insurance policies to a third party even if they were unrelated and didn't have an insurable interest in the insured or the owner of the policy. This landmark ruling made a significant impact on the life insurance industry and set the ball rolling for the birth of the life settlement industry in the United States.

This case involved a patient of Dr. Grigsby's who needed surgery but did not have the funds to pay for the critical operation. The patient agreed to sell Doctor Grigsby his life insurance policy for $100 in exchange for the medical procedure. Doctor Grigsby, therefore, took ownership of the policy and continued to pay the policy's premiums until his patient passed away a year later. When Dr. Grigsby attempted to collect the death benefit, the patient's estate refused to accept the assignment and a court case resulted. The estate's executor challenged the transfer as being void against public policy.

Most thought the executor had a good case as prior U.S. Supreme Court decisions stated that life insurance policies could only be assigned to cover debts and only up to the amount of the obligation. Any insurance coverage greater than that amount was considered a wager and against public policy. It was quite clear that Dr. Grigsby did not have an insurable interest in his patient's life. This controversial case ultimately came before the U.S. Supreme Court where the eminent Justice Oliver Wendell Holmes, Jr., issued the opinion that upheld a policyowner's right of assignment. Dr. Grigsby not only collected the death benefit, he forever changed the life insurance industry in ways that are still benefiting policy holders today.

The Supreme Court. Justice Oliver Wendell Holmes Jr. is the second on the left with quite an impressive mustache.

STACKING THE ODDS IN YOUR FAVOR

Now that life settlements are an advantageous option for so many, thanks to Dr. Grigsby and the Supreme Court, let's look at an important consideration. When seeking a broker to handle your life settlement in a way that benefits you, here are some preliminary questions to ask:

- How can I get the highest fair market value for my policy? Do most of your life insurance policy sales have multiple offers or just one?
- Do you as the broker have a fiduciary duty to me, the policy seller? In other words, do you have my best interest at heart or the buyer's?
- What type of expertise do you, the broker, have that makes the process easier? Do you handle everything from obtaining medical, life expectancy, and policy information to coordinating providers and offers and managing the closing process? Or am I going to have to manage some of that?
- Do you, the broker, have a competitive auction process?
- What happens if my life insurance policy doesn't sell?
- What happens if I get a single, lowball offer?
- Am I automatically disqualified if I'm healthy?

These are the crucial questions that Philip and Gail White asked. This amazing couple has a voracious zest for life and exuberance, especially when you consider they are 82 and 79 years old respectively. They met back in 1975 after they had both been cast in *A Chorus Line*, the box office hit that became the longest-running production in Broadway history until being surpassed by *Cats* in 1997. Phillip and Gail were two of the 17 dancers in the show that went on to win nine Tony Awards.

By 1980, they were married. A leading role on Broadway is not nearly as lucrative as even a supporting role in a television show or movie, but, as Gail points out, "We didn't do Broadway for the money but for the art as well as the prestige." Still, their combined monthly paycheck was plenty hefty, so they're financially independent even though they no longer perform on stage.

They may have given their regards to Broadway, but that doesn't mean they're retired. Although they've lost their ability to perform eye-high kicks, they have certainly not lost their voices. They get hired to entertain large dinner gatherings at corporate events where they sing everyone's favorite Broadway tunes while sharing a bit of the history. It's a terrific way to earn some "fun money" while keeping their passion alive.

In 1997, the Whites purchased a large survivorship universal life policy for estate planning purposes. At that time, the federal estate tax exception was $600,000. This meant that when the second spouse died and the value of their estate was calculated, any amount more than $600,000 would be subject to a federal estate tax of 55 percent. (Just let these numbers sink in for a moment. Yikes!) For years, Gail and Philip discussed the fact that they no longer had a need for this coverage, which had a death benefit of $5,467,985, but they never took action. That was, until they received a notice in the mail that their annual premium would increase to $144,455. With their policy's current cash value of $1,645,504, they decided that it only made sense to surrender it.

Despite the sizeable price tag, their accountant recommended that they consult with our team to confirm that this decision would be the most advantageous. Our first step was to obtain their medical records which enabled us to order a life expectancy (LE) estimate. As Philip and Gail were in relatively good health, the team estimated their LE to be 81 and 90 months. Although this would qualify them for a life settlement, it would not generate more money than the policy's current cash value. In the spirit of perseverance, we ordered a second LE estimate from another company. This additional estimate came back at 53 and 69 months.

Regardless of whether this estimate or the prior one would prove correct, the new LE numbers allowed us to market their policy with confidence that would turn out to be well-founded. Twelve rounds later, we accepted a gross offer of $2.48 million, which was $834,496 greater than the policy's cash value they were going to settle for. Today, they're enjoying this windfall of money, as well as saving $144,455 in annual premium payments, as they continue to perform at gatherings around the country. Can you say five-star hotels?

Making it work

One of the best aspects about the work we do has to be the wonderful people we get to meet along the way. Geoff Singleton, from Saratoga Springs, New York, is no exception. This 83-year-old retired math teacher loved getting his students passionate about mathematics. Many considered him the most popular teacher in the school, partly because so many kids chose to spend their lunchtime in his classroom. While math was his vocation, Geoff truly shone as a track coach. He still runs today at age 84!

When Geoff decided to sell his $1 million universal life policy, he asked for our guidance. None of us were thrilled with the $30,000 offer he received. This was a matter of good news/bad news. Geoff was so fit that potential buyers were concerned he might outlive the policy's maturity date. Our team at Valmark leveraged its relationship with the insurance company that had issued the policy and got them to extend the maturity date. That allowed us to ultimately negotiate an offer of $173,250. This was over five times the original offer.

Tapping expertise and connections

It has been shown time and time again that policy owners, like Geoff, are likely to get more money, even after commissions and fees, because of Valmark's involvement as their life settlement broker. Part of that is because we do whatever we can to make life settlements work. And part of that is, when necessary, we can tap connections that others just don't have. That's what happened with Jamie Purchase, who "suffers" from the same "problem" that Geoff does. As far as potential life insurance policy buyers are concerned, she's too darn healthy.

Jamie, a widow who lives in Whitefish, Montana, loves the outdoors, but her 81-year-old bones are not taking kindly to the frigid cold in the winter months. So, she's considering relocating to Green Valley, Arizona, where many of her friends now live, so she can continue to be as active as possible. She's particularly eager to be able to play pickleball outside year-round and continue to compete in tournaments up and down the West Coast. The proceeds from selling her life insurance will help with this move and lifestyle change, which her two children wholeheartedly support.

In 2000, Jamie had sold the successful marketing firm she had founded years prior. Unfortunately, shortly after selling her business, she experienced financial market crashes that led to prolonged recessions. The last flash crash in March of 2020, when the extent of the pandemic had become a reality, really took a toll on her overall portfolio. It wouldn't have had she stayed the course, but after the markets dropped 34 percent in no time flat, her emotions got the better of her and she liquidated her retirement accounts. We live by the mantra: "It's time in the markets rather than timing the markets." Jaime will be fine and will not outlive her assets, but her once vast fortune is no longer what it used to be.

Since estate taxes are no longer an issue, the $2 million trust-owned life insurance policy her husband had purchased in 2011 for estate planning purposes is no longer part of her plan. Thoughts about divesting herself of the life insurance were recently reinforced when her insurance company notified her that her annual premiums would be increasing to $90,613. That's a lot of money to keep an unnecessary policy in force.

As there was zero cash surrender value remaining in the policy, Jamie's plan was to let the policy lapse and walk away with zero dollars. Luckily, one of our clients in Arizona mentioned life settlements during a conversation and, subsequently, referred Jamie to our team, where we once again came across that good news/bad news scenario. The good news for Jamie is that she is very healthy with a life expectancy (LE) of 161 months. The not-so-good news when it came to selling her policy was that her LE was 161 months, which meant her policy was not easily marketable on the secondary market. Instead of turning her away, however, we knew from experience that her age and the aspects of her policy could be enticing to a specialty provider that purchases policies on healthy insureds. We were able to obtain a gross offer on her policy for $210,000.

Choose wisely

Clearly, who you're working with can make a huge difference. You want to make sure you've lined up the best possible team to handle what can be a complicated, time-consuming process. That means that you—or the financial professional you work with—needs to ask the kinds of questions we provided above. That goes double for checking credentials, which we'll talk about next.

- BUCKET LIST
- BOULDER
- CUBA
- BONGOS
- DEPT. OF INSURANCE
- WILL ROGERS

Chapter 6

PROTECTING YOURSELF OR YOUR CLIENT

Your Best Interest Needs to Be the Priority

Confidence ... thrives on honesty, on honor, on the sacredness of obligations, on faithful protection, and on unselfish performance. Without them it cannot live.
—Franklin D. Roosevelt

We know that life settlements, by definition, are a delicate business. Not only do you have to consider your mortality, but you also need to make sure you're aligning yourself with the team positioned to get you the best deal.

But wait, there's more! You also need to make sure that you—or your client—are not being taken for a nasty ride by someone who has their best interest at heart rather than yours.

Taking all these steps to check credentials may sound like overkill, but not so much. So, we're going to give you—or the financial professional you work with—a bit more homework when it comes to making sure the people you hire to potentially sell your life insurance policy have the right stuff.

That's exactly what Andrew Chen did.

Even after learning about the ins and outs of life settlements, Andrew, a 55-year-old successful financial advisor from Boulder, Colorado, still had concerns. Andrew, a.k.a. the money man, was a true advocate for comprehensive planning and building strong relationships with his clients, which he referred to as extended family members.

Since Andrew has a passion for international travel and music, his walls are covered with photos of musicians he's come across on the trips he's taken. He also has a set of bongos that he acquired on a trip to Cuba in the early '90s. Before U.S. citizens were allowed to travel freely to the small island nation, Andrew discovered the backdoor route via Mexico, and decided to take a three-month sabbatical in eastern Cuba, where the majority of the population consists of Afro-Cubans and where bongos originated. Intrigued by their simplicity, he bought a set and quickly became proficient on them. By the time he returned to work, they had become an extension of Andrew's persona. So, naturally, he moved them into his office, and has even been known to play for his favorite clients.

Recently, Andrew had his annual physical and after several tests he received the unthinkable news that he has stage 4 cancer. In shock and disbelief for the first couple of months, he continued working, trying to hide his pain but with limited success. Clients noticed the spark was no longer present in his eyes. Finally, with the help of a Living with Dying support group for terminally ill patients, he began to come to terms with his diagnosis, and after a few sessions, was able to open up to his business partners, staff, and clients about the limited time he had left.

With time no longer on his side, Andrew drew up a bucket list of travel destinations. He had recognized that it was time to sell his shares in the partnership.

Although the partners understood and sympathized with his decision to retire early, the firm had overextended itself, having recently acquired two other firms in Denver and Colorado Springs. These transactions had tied up the firm's resources which meant Andrew would not be able to liquidate his shares anytime soon. Then they remembered that, years ago, the practice had purchased insurance on Andrew's life to fulfill their buy/sell agreement.

The partners were referred to our team, and after reviewing all the viable options they had, it was mutually determined that selling this policy and obtaining a life settlement was the only way they would be able to buy Andrew out. Our team brought in multiple providers through our auction process. After six rounds of bidding, we negotiated a settlement offer, resulting in a total gross offer of $1.28 million. The policy was a term nonconvertible with a death benefit of $1.75 million and no cash surrender value. So, after taxes and commissions, the firm had enough money to purchase Andrew's shares in the business, and Andrew had enough money to not only travel first class with his bongos, but also to live out the remainder of his life with financial peace of mind.

Like so many professionals who work in the financial arena, Andrew and his partners had never heard of life settlements. Like many people, he was initially skeptical, especially since his only knowledge of the life settlement process was from an article he had read on the impact and legal issues related to STOLI—stranger-owned life insurance policy. This is a ploy used to take advantage of the life settlement process. Those who originally participated and promoted the idea persuaded senior citizens to apply for large life insurance policies with the intention of only holding the policy past the contestability period, typically two years, and then selling the policy through the life settlement process.

The insured senior citizen would receive a nonrecourse loan, enough to cover annual premiums, using the life insurance as collateral. The lure for participants was free life insurance for a couple of years, or until the policy was sold, upfront payout, and an additional payout after the life settlement process was complete. It has been documented that the insureds were instructed to make false health or financial information on the application. Once the STOLI policies came to light, lawsuits were quick to follow, brought by the insured and the insurance companies as they began rescinding the policies for misrepresentation and lack of insurable interest. Because of the STOLI fiasco, policies entering the life settlement process must be seasoned (meaning they've been accumulating contributions in the owner's account, typically for at least two years) and purchased for legitimate reasons.

As of 2022, 43 states and the territory of Puerto Rico regulate life settlements through each state's Department of Insurance. Thirty of them have a mandated holding period of two years before selling a life insurance policy, and 11 states have a five-year waiting period; Minnesota is the only state with a four-year holding period.[21] Some exceptions allow a policy owner to sell their policy before the holding period is complete if they meet certain criteria (i.e., the owner/insured's chronic or terminal illness, divorce, retirement, physical or mental disability, etc.).

Regulations vary from state to state, but the majority require a life settlement-approved agent and broker-dealer to act in the seller's interest, with the buyer being represented by a provider licensed by the state. In addition, most states require that documents used in the selling process be approved to make sure they are coherent, understandable, and fair. Additional regulations determined by state officials are not uncommon and range from placing the funds in escrow accounts to spelling out when the funds can be released to the seller.

Voluntary scrutiny

Despite these safeguards, the life settlement arena can still be compromised by unethical behavior or people out to get the most money for themselves rather than for those selling their life insurance policies. So, Valmark maintains procedures designed to guard against fraudulent behavior, which revolve around knowing the intricate details of the clients as well as the multiple insurance providers involved in the bidding process.

For starters, our Valmark team is composed of life settlement brokers, which means they're all licensed and have a professional duty to do right by the person who wants to sell the policy as opposed to the potential buyer of the life insurance policy.

In addition, we are the only company that treats each life settlement as a security transaction, which voluntarily opens the door for additional scrutiny and compliance regulations. By doing so, we reduce the risk for those who participate in the life settlement process. In addition, our unique compliance-oriented proprietary system, The Life Settlement Advocacy Program™, guides members along the process, creating the highest value for their life insurance policy.

What does this mean for you?

When a company works in your best interest, things tend to work out in your favor. When it comes to life settlements, that means that you get the best possible price for your policy.

The information on the regulation of life settlements reassured financial advisor Andrew Chen. Finding out about our fiduciary duty was downright encouraging. Still, he wanted to know how to keep himself—and even more so his clients—safe from fraud as well as how to maintain privacy. That's something you need to know as well.

How do I maintain my privacy?

Maintaining privacy when selling your life insurance policy is a general concern shared by others who have sold their policies to investors. It's not uncommon for the new policy owner to contact you or your designated agent periodically from the time you sell your life insurance policy until later years to confirm your address and check on your health status. Most states limit such interactions to once every three months until the year before your life expectancy, at which point they may contact you monthly. Depending on the closing arrangements, the new policy owner may have the right to demand that you produce updated medical records if you haven't signed a HIPAA release to access updated records (which most new owners will typically ask for). Upon your passing, your estate executor or heirs will be required to produce a copy of your death certificate to the new policy owner so that the policy death benefits can be filed with the insurance provider. Until then, however, you certainly don't want to have some stranger with a vested interest in your demise pestering you about how you're feeling.

That's why reputable life settlement companies will make sure to safeguard your privacy right from the start. Here's what Valmark has to say about that:

> Valmark works exclusively with institutional and accredited investors. They typically hold your policy in a double-blind trust with hundreds or even thousands of other policies. This helps assure the client that their information remains confidential. The investor participates in the performance of the portfolio, which contains numerous policies. It operates like a bond portfolio where the investor is less concerned about each bond but rather the overall performance of the pool of assets.
>
> Valmark places the protection of personal information as a top priority. During the transaction, our privacy policy and confidential process will ensure that no information leaves any of the authorized parties working on the case. Both Valmark and our approved accredited purchasers follow strict HIPAA guidelines to safeguard your personal information. After the transaction, your policy will be managed in a double-blind corporate trust and personal information will continue to be secure according to HIPAA guidelines.

That was good enough for Andrew Chen. Once he had satisfied himself that privacy concerns could be addressed when the right people with the right expertise handled a life settlement, he was left with only one question: How could he determine whether they really knew their stuff and whether they would understand—and be able to explain—the financial implications when selling a policy? Not surprisingly, since he's a financial advisor, tax consequences are always top of mind for Andrew. They're also something that everyone considering a life settlement should be informed about.

THE TAX MAN

As Will Rogers said, "The difference between death and taxes is death doesn't get worse every time Congress meets." You never want to let the tax tail wag the dog, but it's important to understand the tax ramifications when determining whether selling your life insurance policy is the best option, especially since life settlement transactions are taxed in different ways. Let's look at an example based on a gross payout of $500,000. You'll find explanations directly below the chart, so don't worry if it seems confusing at first glance.

- All premiums that you've paid into the policy over the years to cover the cost of insurance come back to you tax-free. These are considered the tax basis. In this example, $200,000 of the $500,000 windfall would have no taxes due.
- Any cash surrender value that the policy had is taxed at ordinary income tax rates. Assuming a 32 percent tax bracket, $16,000 would go to Uncle Sam.
- Any life settlement proceeds that exceed the cash surrender value will be taxed at the capital gains tax rate.

Assuming a 23.8 percent tax rate, $59,500 would also be paid in taxes.
- In this illustration, there would be a tax burden of $75,500. The remaining $424,500 would be the moolah you get to take home.

When considering moving forward with a life settlement, we strongly suggest that you or your client speak to a tax advisor before making any decisions regarding a life settlement. Keep in mind that, in addition to taxes, there will be fees paid to the team representing you through this extended and intricate process.

How Does Uncle Sam Tax a Life Settlement?
An Example of a $500,000 Life Settlement

$200,000	$50,000	$250,000
Cost of Insurance Insurance Payments	Cash Surrender Value Residual	Life Settlement Proceeds Above Cash Surrender
Tax Free!	Ordinary Income $16,000 assuming a 32% tax rate.	Capital Gains $59,500 assuming a 23.8% tax rate.

Taxes Paid: $75,500.
After Tax Payout: $424,500.

Compensation

Understandably, there is a cost for having a team organize, auction, and negotiate the sale of your policy. Andrew Chen was clear on that; his clients, after all, paid him a fee for the services he provided to them. He likes to say, "Costs only become an objection in the absence of value."

As Andrew learned and as you're likely figuring out having made it almost to the end of this book, life settlement transactions are complex, time intensive, and have significant expenditures. It's not uncommon for a life team to receive fees up to 30 percent of the gross offer. While it's imperative to know what the fees are in advance and how they're determined, it also helps to remember that, ultimately, 70 percent of something is better than 100 percent of nothing.

Transparency

Ascertaining—and nailing down—the agent/broker compensation is just the start when it comes to the kind of transparency you want to look for. Luckily, transparency has become an important component of life settlement regulation across the country. For example, recent legislation actually mandates full disclosure of compensation paid to brokers along with notification of all bids, counteroffers, and rejections during the bid process. In addition, most states mandate that clients be informed about settlement alternatives, taxation, and government aid concerns, as well as the licensing of life settlement agents, brokers, and providers.

Hopefully, all the above information will come your way as a matter of course. If it doesn't, at least you now know what to ask for. In addition, you will want to make sure that your agent/

broker negotiates any received offers using a formal written bid process. There's truly no way of knowing which providers will extend the strongest bids at any given time. In order to receive top dollar for a life insurance policy, it's critical to have a formal, systematic, and written procedure in place that works in accordance with an auction-like process. This allows all providers to compete on a level playing field and awards cases solely on the merits of the buyer making the most beneficial offer and indicates to the sellers that they are receiving true fair market value for the sale of their policies. There have been cases where the initial offer is only 25 percent of the final offer after the formal bidding process was complete. You certainly want to make sure that no one grabs that first offer on your behalf just because that's the easiest and fastest course of action.

GETTING IT RIGHT

This brings us back to Andrew Chen. After all the due diligence he had done, he was 99 percent convinced that he had found the right team to work with. Then he found out that he and his firm would have the opportunity to change their mind—even at the last possible moment. In fact, even after that. If circumstances somehow changed and a life settlement was no longer the best option for Andrew and the firm, he would be in control and not obligated to agree to an offer. That changes once an offer has been accepted and the transaction is in process. At that point, Andrew and his firm would have to check with his state laws to determine the latest date a seller can rescind the offer and walk away from the transaction without penalties. Until then, however, Andrew realized he had the prerogative to back out. With that, Andrew's last bit of lingering doubt about the team he had chosen was erased.

For the right people, life settlements can be the answer to a prayer—as long as they're handled in the right way. That means that if you're going to consider selling your life insurance policy, you absolutely have to consult an expert with the necessary chops whose priority is doing right by you.

Conclusion

IS A LIFE INSURANCE SETTLEMENT FOR YOU?

> *"Today is your day! Your mountain is waiting; so ... get on your way!"*
> —Dr. Seuss

A little—or a lot—of extra cash can come in handy, so it's not the least bit surprising that people who don't need their life insurance any longer are opting to trade it in. Even businesses are getting in on the action.

No wonder life settlements are starting to look like the next big thing on the financial front. Forecasting predicted that the face value of all life settlement policies sold would be $1.8 billion, but in 2021 it was about $4 billion.[22] That growth makes total sense when you consider a life settlement can often deliver a lovely windfall to people still paying for life insurance policies that life circumstances have rendered unnecessary.

In this book, you have met a wide variety of our clients. Their stories represent just a few of a slew of potential situations where life insurance had once played a pivotal role in providing security and peace of mind. Years—or decades—later, however, the need for such coverage has diminished or evaporated altogether.

Most people believe they have only three options for their now unwanted and unneeded life insurance policies. You can:

- Retain the insurance coverage and the policy and continue paying the increased premiums
- Restructure the coverage and premium
- Surrender the policy for its cash value or simply walk away

And yet today there is a fourth option that might benefit you—or your client—much more. You can potentially profit from the sale of your life insurance policy. You know, of course, that your home, automobile, boat, investment portfolio, investment real estate, and business interests are all considered capital assets. Now you're aware that your life insurance policies are also considered a capital asset—an asset that may have significant value.

Interested in exploring the possibility of a life settlement? Getting started couldn't be easier. If this were a musical, it would be called *Three Simple Steps*. We'll spare you the song and dance (trust us, you don't want to see those from us) and just give you the scoop. All you have to do is:

1. **Contact us for an initial review**
   - Name
   - Date of birth
   - Brief summary of your situation and life insurance policy details

2. **We help you gather necessary documents**
   - In-force policy illustration (a presentation or depiction of how the policy's cash value should perform over time)
   - Current life insurance policy information
   - A summary of your health information

3. **We prepare a policy evaluation**
   - Preliminary estimate of market value
   - Consult with you about the case
   - Determine how to move forward

As we've seen over and over, you must be in the know to make a decision that will best serve you and your family or your client. So, we've put together a brief quiz to help you determine how well you understand this whole business of life settlements and whether you or your client might be a candidate. Don't worry, we're not going to grade you. We wouldn't even if we could see your answers, which, of course, we can't.

Okay, here goes:

1. **Up to what percentage of life insurance policies never pay a death benefit because they expire, lapse, or are surrendered?**
   - 20 percent
   - 45 percent
   - 72 percent
   - 90 percent

   Shockingly, up to 90 percent of life insurance policies[23] never pay a death benefit. Instead, they become void due to the expiration date or lack of payment, or people surrendering them for pennies on the dollar.

2. **If I don't need my life insurance policy anymore and don't want to keep paying the premiums, should I just walk away or is there another option?**
Most people believe they have only three options for their now unwanted and unneeded life insurance policies: 1) Keep the policy and continue paying the increased premiums. 2) Decrease the death benefit of the policy to maintain an affordable premium. 3) Let the policy lapse and receive any potential cash value that has accumulated if it's a permanent policy or simply walk away. But there's a fourth option. A life settlement may allow you to sell your unneeded life insurance policy to a third party.

3. **If I get a life settlement, will my beneficiaries still collect a death benefit from the life insurance policy I sold?**
It's important to keep in mind that once you have transferred ownership of your policy to another entity or investor, your beneficiaries will no longer have a death benefit to collect upon your death.

4. **Could a life settlement have any financial consequences other than my potentially receiving money for my life insurance policy?**
There are tax consequences to a life settlement transaction as the proceeds from the sale of a policy may be subject to state or federal taxes. Before entering into a life settlement, check with a tax professional about the tax implications of any transaction you are considering. In addition, receiving a large payout could adversely affect one's eligibility for

state or federal public assistance, such as Medicaid or other governmental programs. And your ability to purchase additional insurance in the future may be diminished or no longer available as your old policy will still be in force, you just don't own it anymore. This may affect your ability to get additional coverage. Even if you can get a new policy, you may have to pay higher premiums because of your age or changes in your health status. So, before you proceed with a life settlement, be sure you fully understand the financial implications.

5. **Does getting a life settlement cost anything?**
   In addition to taxes, life settlements can have transaction costs of up to 30 percent. These are paid out of the gross revenue from the sale of policies. It is important to have these fees disclosed in writing before you sign on with a life settlement broker. Of course, it's helpful to remember that ending up with 70 percent of something is better than getting 100 percent of nothing.

6. **Are all life settlement brokers the same?**
   No. You want to look for a broker who is licensed and has a desire to work in the best interest of the person who wants to sell the policy as opposed to the potential buyer of the life insurance policy.

7. **Should I explore the possibility of a life settlement if I no longer need my life insurance for estate planning purposes or to protect my spouse, my heirs, or my income?**
   Absolutely. Why keep paying for a life insurance policy you've outgrown the need for? Besides, you can change

your mind even after an offer to buy your life insurance policy has been made. So, you're not locked into anything until you accept the offer. Depending on the state you live in, there may even be some wiggle room at that point.

8. **I'm 72. Despite the recent diagnosis of a medical condition, the doctor says I have a good 10 years to live. Am I a potential life settlement candidate?**

    Yes, you are. Here are the prerequisites:

    - *The insured's age is 65 or older, unless you're facing a life-shortening condition*
    - *There has been a decline in health from the original policy issue and their life expectancy is 15 years or less (but as you've read, our team has secured life settlements for some perfectly healthy individuals so take this part with a grain of salt)*
    - *The life insurance policy has a net death benefit of $250,000 or more (there's no maximum)*
    - *The policy owner can be an individual, trust, or corporation*
    - *Life insurance policies can be universal life, guaranteed universal life, survivorship universal life, variable universal life, and convertible term. Flexible premium policies like universal life are more favored by buyers because they can readily adjust the premiums going forward.*
    - *The annual premium should be 5 percent of the death benefit (or less), and the cash surrender value should be 15 percent of the death benefit (or less)*

How'd you do on the quiz?

Do you feel that you have a solid understanding about life settlements and that you could be a candidate? Give us a call at our office or email us to chat about your options.

Do you still have questions about life settlements? Give us a call at our office or email us to discuss the possibilities.

Just want to introduce yourself and talk? Give us a call at our office or email us.

Yes, we like to have fun, and we hope we've brought some levity to a serious topic. However, we take our roles as advisors seriously. We're as passionate about helping people as we are about life. Our goal is to help people live the life they have always imagined in their years of financial independence.

When the time is right for you, we look forward to meeting you. Just remember the words we quoted from Warren Miller earlier in the book:

If you don't do it this year, you'll be one year older when you do.

Cheers to you!

David Rosell & Rodney Cook

The offices of Rosell Wealth Management

550 NW Franklin Ave, Ste 368
Bend, OR 97703
(541) 390-3832

david@rosellwealthmanagement.com
rodney@rosellwealthmanagement.com

www.RosellWealthManagement.com

FOR CPAS, ATTORNEYS, AND INSURANCE AGENTS:
Want to know more about life settlements and potentially receive CE credits while you're at it? Book a one-hour Zoom conference with us.

David addresses international audiences numbering in the thousands including the Million Dollar Round Table®.

To inquire about having David speak at your event, please email: speaking@RosellWealthManagement.com

David **ROSELL**
AUTHOR | SPEAKER | WEALTH MANAGER

LIFE SETTLEMENTS ARE NOT ALL WE DO!

If you are at or near retirement, you have already accumulated some wealth, you know how much money you have, but you don't have a clear picture of what your money can or can't do for you for the remainder of your life, feel free to begin a dialogue at:

www.RosellWealthManagement.com
david@rosellwealthmanagement.com
(541) 385-8831

OTHER BOOKS BY DAVID ROSELL

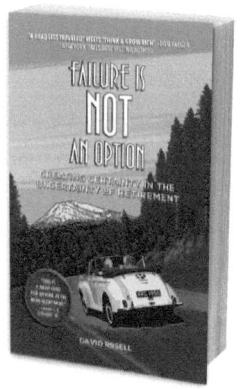

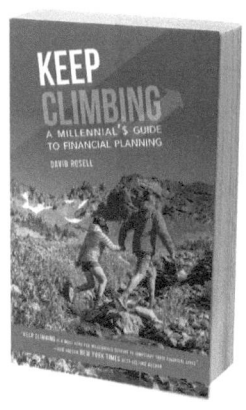

Countless books exist to tell you how to accumulate wealth and get out of debt. Few resources, however, teach what to do once you have reached the top, even though you are faced with unique and potentially devastating risks as you begin the second half of your financial journey. This book fills that gap. Through an unexpected melding of travel and family stories coupled with financial survival tips, *Failure Is Not an Option* lays out the eight fundamental risks every retiree faces in retirement. In the process, this book will help you achieve far greater financial certainty and peace of mind.

"If you're at or near retirement, this is a must-read. *Failure Is Not an Option* provides a compass for making the most of the second half of your financial journey. After reading David Rosell's book, you'll want to explore all that life has to offer."
—Charles R. Schwab, Jr.

"David Rosell's guide to retirement planning shows you not only how to get your finances in order, but also how to bring meaning and purpose to these very special years."
—Ken Blanchard, co-author of T*he One Minute Manager*® and *Trust Works!*

"This powerful, practical book gives you a step-by-step guide to retiring in comfort and never worrying about money again."
—Brian Tracy, author of *Change Your Thinking, Change Your Life*

"I have always said there are three ingredients in the good life: learning, earning, and being hungry. Read *Failure Is Not an Option*. David Rosell has the recipe to create the retirement you envision with no limitations."
—Les Brown, motivational speaker and author of *You've Got to Be Hungry*

"David Rosell is the perfect coach for the training phase of life we call retirement."
—Ashton Eaton, 2012 Olympic Gold Medal in decathlon, current world record holder in the decathlon and heptathlon events.

"*The Road Less Traveled* meets *Think and Grow Rich*. Achieving greatness in your retirement years can now be available to all of us after reading *Failure Is Not an Option*."
—Don Yaeger, *New York Times* bestselling author, former associate editor of *Sports Illustrated*

"*Failure Is Not an Option* provides the game plan to not only survive but to thrive!"
—Ed Viesturs, America's foremost high-altitude mountaineer, National Geographic's Adventurer of the Year, motivational speaker, and author of *No Shortcuts to the Top*

ABOUT DAVID ROSELL

David's inspiration and zest for life have been shaped by a lifetime of international adventures. To date, he has traveled to more than 75 countries on six different continents.

David is the founder and president of Rosell Wealth Management, an entrepreneurial firm located in Bend, Oregon. For more than 20 years, he has specialized in working with affluent individuals and families who are at or near retirement, helping them live the life they have always imagined.

About David Rosell

As a recipient of the Retirement Distribution Certificate from the University of Pennsylvania's Wharton School of Business, David excels in making complicated financial planning topics easy to understand. An accomplished speaker, he has addressed international audiences numbering in the thousands, including the Million Dollar Roundtable® and Vistage Worldwide.

David is the host of the podcast Recession-Proof Your Retirement and author of two other entertaining books that meld his passions for adventure and finance: Failure Is NOT an Option: Creating Certainty in the Uncertainty of Retirement and Keep Climbing: A Millennial's Guide to Financial Planning. He has been featured on CNN Money, NBC News, Fox Business, MSN Money, and NPR, and in the Chicago Tribune, U.S. News & World Report, The New York Daily News, and Yahoo Finance.

His life in Bend, Oregon, and Jackson, Wyoming, is constantly inspired by his two children, Sophie and Jack, who are becoming seasoned travelers themselves. When he's not working or parenting, David indulges in writing from his motorhome named Bennie, downhill skiing, mountain biking, and paddleboarding as well as traveling with his partner, Heather.

David was the first Oregon professional licensed to offer life settlements.

ABOUT RODNEY COOK

Rodney's passions can be summed up in three words: *family*, *service*, and *adventure*.

Rodney is a partner and director of financial planning at Rosell Wealth Management, a firm located in beautiful Bend, Oregon, that exclusively works with owners getting ready to sell their business and individuals and families as they prepare for—and then enter—retirement.

About Rodney Cook

As a Certified Financial Planner™ (CFP) and a recipient of the Private Wealth Advisor certificate from the Yale School of Management, Rodney specializes in helping successful people who are at or near retirement to achieve their retirement goals. With a history of mastering the most advanced knowledge and techniques to address the sophisticated needs of his clients, he has become an expert on life settlements. Rodney's mantra comes from the words of his favorite motivational speaker, Les Brown: "Help others achieve their dreams, and you will achieve yours." An advocate for our youth, Rodney is a board member for Friends of the Children, a nationwide long-term mentorship program for the most at-risk youth in our communities. He is also a mentor for the CFP board, helping young professionals navigate the investment service industry.

As avid adventure seekers, Rodney, his wife Kira, and son Makaih enjoy mountain biking, trail running, and hiking on the trails around Bend. In the winter, you will find them skiing and snowmobiling high in the mountains, and in the summer, flying around the lakes on their Jet Skis and looking for the next trail to conquer. Rodney and Kira have a goal to have run or mountain biked on trails in 60 different countries by the age of 60.

Rodney is a true lover of life, people, and living to the fullest! He is an integral part of Rosell Wealth Management, the first Oregon firm licensed to offer life settlements.

NOTES

1. https://faculty.wharton.upenn.edu/wp-content/uploads/2016/11/Insurance41.pdf
2. https://www.taxpolicycenter.org/briefing-book/how-many-people-pay-estate-tax - Change stat to 99.9 percent.
3. https://www.wealthmanagement.com/insurance/survey-shows-life-settlements-remain-misunderstood
4. https://www.wealthmanagement.com/insurance/survey-shows-life-settlements-remain-misunderstood
5. https://lewisellis.com/industry-insights/article/40044757-many-seniors-still-see-life-insurance-policies-lapse
6. http://lewisellis.com/industry-insights/article/40044757-many-seniors-still-see-life-insurance-policies-lapse
7. Valmark Securities, "Creating Value out of an Existing Life Insurance Policy" brochure
8. https://www.wealthmanagement.com/insurance/why-insurance-companies-want-stop-life-settlements
9. https://lecp.naifa.org/what-you-should-know-about-life-insurance-settlements
10. https://blog.lisa.org/advisor/combating-inflation-with-life-settlement-earnings/
11. https://www.thinkadvisor.com/2015/04/02/on-the-rebound-advisors-see-big-dollars-in-life-settlements-2/
12. https://lewisellis.com/industry-insights/article/40044757-many-seniors-still-see-life-insurance-policies-lapse
13. The Deal.com
14. The Life Settlements Report released by The Deal
15. https://www.irs.gov/businesses/small-businesses-self-employed/estate-tax
16. https://www.irs.gov/businesses/small-businesses-self-employed/estate-tax
17. https://taxfoundation.org/federal-estate-and-gift-tax-rates-exemptions-and-exclusions-1916-2014/
18. https://blog.lisa.org/advisor/combating-inflation-with-life-settlement-earnings/

19. https://www.worlddata.info/america/venezuela/inflation-rates.php
20. https://www.bls.gov/news.release/cpi.nr0.htm
21. https://supreme.justia.com/cases/federal/us/222/149/
22. https://blog.lisa.org/member/find-out-which-states-have-life-and-viatical-settlement-regulations/
23. The Deal.com
24. https://faculty.wharton.upenn.edu/wp-content/uploads/2016/11/Insurance41.pdf